NUTSHELLS

CONSUMER LAW IN A NUTSHELL

AUSTRALIA
Law Book Co.
Sydney

CANADA and USA
Carswell
Toronto

HONG KONG
Sweet & Maxwell Asia

NEW ZEALAND
Brookers
Auckland

SINGAPORE and MALAYSIA
Sweet & Maxwell Asia
Singapore and Kuala Lumpur

NUTSHELLS

CONSUMER LAW
IN A NUTSHELL

FOURTH EDITION

by

Sandra Silberstein, LL.B (Hons)
Solicitor and Senior Lecturer in Law,
Leeds Metropolitan University

London • Sweet & Maxwell • 2004

Published in 2004 by Sweet & Maxwell Limited of
100 Avenue Road, Swiss Cottage, London, NW3 3PF
Typeset by LBJ Typesetting Ltd of Kingsclere
Printed & bound by Creative Print & Design, Wales

No natural forests were destroyed to make this product;
only farmed timber was used and replanted

A CIP Catalogue record for this book is available
from the British Library

ISBN 0 421 787 406

©
Sweet & Maxwell
2004

*To Martin, Daniel, Rebecca and Deborah
with much love.*

CONTENTS

1. CONSUMER TRANSACTIONS GOVERNED BY THE SALE OF GOODS ACT 1979

Every consumer transaction is based on the law of contract. The consumer is agreeing to purchase goods or services and the seller in return is to provide them. Therefore, every consumer law student must ensure that they understand the basics of contract law before moving onto the special rules and statutes governing consumer law. The major Act that assists consumers is the Sale of Goods Act 1979 as amended by the Sale and Supply of Goods Act 1994 and the Sale and Supply of Goods to Consumers Regulations 2002. In this book all references are to the sections in the 1979 Act as amended by these two pieces of legislation. The Sale of Goods Act 1979 governs all transactions where "goods" are transferred for a monetary consideration called the price.

The definition of goods

The word "goods" is defined by section 61 of the Act, and includes all personal chattels, but not money unless it is a curio or an antique, and things attached to, or forming part of, the land that are agreed to be severed before sale.

Consideration

The consideration has to be a monetary consideration (note *Esso Petroleum Co. Ltd v Customs and Excise Commissioners* (1976)) so that if a consumer merely "swaps or exchanges goods" then the transaction cannot be covered by the Sale of Goods Act 1979. (It will in fact be governed by the Supply of Goods and Services Act 1982, see later p.24.)

However, where the consumer hands over goods in part exchange and adds cash to make up the balance, then irrespective of the amount of cash, the transaction is governed by the Sale of Goods Act. (See *e.g. Aldridge v Johnson* (1857).) Therefore, if Joe Bloggs part-exchanges his £4,000 car against a car costing £7,000 and adds £3,000 cash, the transaction is covered by the Sale of Goods Act.

Conditions implied into the contract

Once it is established that the transaction is governed by the Act, the following conditions are implied into the contract. Naturally, the consumer may well have asked and agreed certain terms about the goods, in which case some matters may have become express terms of the contract as well as applying the implied conditions. The significance of the fact that these are implied conditions will be dealt with later when remedies are considered.

Sale by description

In every contract for the sale of goods, section 13 of the Act states that where there is a sale of goods by description there is an implied condition that the goods will correspond with their description.

What is a sale by description?

(a) Ten rolls of ready-pasted vinyl wallpaper from a larger consignment Batch No.1234.
(b) Sales of specific goods that the buyer has not seen but is relying on the description supplied. (Note: *e.g. Varley v Whipp*, below.)
(c) Sales of specific goods which the buyer has seen if they are sold as goods answering a description, *e.g.* 2004 Ford Focus 10,000 miles.
(d) Sales in supermarkets where the buyer selects the goods.

Section 13 applies to all sales both by private individuals and businesses so all sellers are caught by its provisions.

(**Note**: *Varley v Whipp* (1900)—private sale of second hand reaping machine, described as new the previous year. The machine was obviously not new the previous year. This was a sale by description, so the buyer was entitled to reject as the goods did not match their description.)

Beale v Taylor (1967)

Sale of car described as Herald Convertible White, 1961. The buyer inspected the car and purchased it. In fact the car was two halves welded together, the back of it being a 1200 1961 Herald convertible, and the front part being an earlier model. The Court of Appeal held that this was a sale by description. The argument was put forward by the seller that the buyer was buying specific goods and had inspected them. This, he argued, prevented them from being a sale by description. The court rejected this. The buyer was entitled to a remedy and was awarded £125, being the price less the scrap value.

Supermarket sales

The condition applies to the purchase of all goods selected by the buyer in supermarkets. See section 13(3), which states that a sale of goods is not prevented from being a sale by description by reason only that being exposed for sale or hire they are selected by the buyer. Therefore, if the consumer selects goods from the supermarket shelf described as peaches, or 100 per cent wool sweater, and the tin turns out to contain pears and the sweater to be a wool mixture with acrylic, there has been a breach of this condition. Nowadays as we move into an era where shoppers select their own goods from large stores and hypermarkets without help from sales assistants but relying on signs and packaging, this section assumes a high level of importance. Television and cable shopping channels and the growth in consumer purchasing over the internet will also add to its significance.

Reliance

There must be some reliance by the buyer on the words that form part of the description for it to be a sale by description. In a commercial case, *Reardon Smith v Hansen Tangen* (1976), the House of Lords held that the mark of identification given to an oil tanker did not form part of the description (it was unimportant and no reliance had been placed on it). In *Harlingdon & Leinster v Christopher Hull Fine Art* (1991), the Court of Appeal decided that in a transaction between two art dealers, the buyer had not relied on the description so it was not a sale by description. The seller had attempted to make it clear he was not an expert in a particular field of painting and that the buyer bought the painting "at his own risk". It should also be noted this was a highly specialised sale of goods where the buyer could be judged to be more of an expert than the seller, a situation that does not normally arise in the majority of consumer sales.

However, in standard consumer cases, the buyer will rely heavily on the description *e.g.* 100 per cent wool sweater; 2004 Nissan Micra, 1,000 miles; and the problem of it not being a sale by description because of lack of reliance on the description will not normally arise. The sale of a yacht in *Clegg v Olle Andersson* (2003) "with a shoal draught keel in accordance with the manufacturer's standard specification", was a sale by description.

Section 13(2) states that if the sale is by sample as well as by description it is not sufficient that the bulk of the goods correspond with the sample, if the goods do not correspond with the description. This is especially useful in furniture sales where consumers are likely to choose from samples. If the carpet is described as 100 per cent wool, even if the customer is given the same carpet as the sample, if the carpet is not 100 per cent wool there is a breach of this condition.

In *Arcos Ltd v Ronaasen* (1933) the goods in question were described as "half inch wooden staves". Five per cent of the consignment, which was delivered, was half an inch thick, many staves were between half an inch–9/16" thick, and many more were wider still. Lord Atkin made his famous speech in this case when ordering to such specific quantities:

> "A ton does not mean about a ton, or a yard about a yard. Still less, when you descend to minute measurements, does half an inch mean about half an inch? IF THE SELLER WANTS A MARGIN HE MUST STIPULATE FOR IT."

The buyer was therefore entitled to reject as the goods did not match their description.

Thus this case could be extremely useful for the consumer do-it-yourself person, but Lord Atkin's comments must be noted and many retailers stipulate a fairly generous tolerance level nowadays.

Remedies

Section 13 is a condition that means that the buyer is able in terms of a remedy to reject the goods and obtain a refund. Some examples below illustrate how the buyer can benefit from this. Particularly useful in terms of a remedy is section 30 of the Sale of Goods Act 1979, which states what a consumer buyer can do when he ends up with different quantities from what was ordered. Because a different amount has been obtained, there has been a breach of description.

Too many goods delivered

What happens if the seller sends too many of the goods ordered, *e.g.* three pan sets instead of one? The buyer can reject all three sets, or keep the one he ordered and return the other two, or he can keep all three, paying for them at the contract rate. (Section 30(2) and (3).)

Too few goods delivered

The buyer is not obliged to accept delivery by instalments unless he has agreed. If a lesser amount arrives, he can reject them or keep them. If he does keep them, then he has to pay a proportion of the contract rate so that if three pan sets have been ordered and only one is delivered, the buyer can keep that one or reject it. (Section 30(1).)

Other remedies issues

In cases where a breach of description is involved, students ought always to consider the possibility of a misrepresentation arising. Also, to be discussed later, is possible criminal liability for the retailer under the Trade Descriptions Act 1968.

---

2. LIABILITY FOR DEFECTIVE GOODS

The major problem facing consumers is that the goods they have purchased turn out to be defective; the cooker breaks down after a month; the television set blows up; the sweater shrinks to half its size after being washed correctly.

What assistance does the 1979 Act afford consumers?

Section 14 starts where goods are sold in the course of a business, so it only covers the situation when the retailer is in business. It does not cover private sales. However, it should be noted the status of the buyer is irrelevant. Section 14 applies to business buyers as well as to private buyers.

Section 14 only applies to sales made "in the course of a business"

Section 61 of the Act says that in the course of a business includes a profession and the activities of any government department or local or public authority. For consumers, the phrase "in the course of a business" normally presents few problems. Sales by stores, garages or mail order are obviously made in the course of a business and it makes no difference that the seller was handling a particular kind of product for the first time. In *Stevenson v Rogers* (1998), the defendant fisherman sold his only fishing vessel to the buyer. Although the defendant did not normally sell fishing boats and it was a "one-off" sale, it was held to be a sale in the course of a business, so the implied conditions in section 14 applied. This case and recent amendments made by the 2002 Regulations suggest that, certainly under the civil law, any sale or purchase of goods by a business will be made in the course of a business regardless of whether the sale or purchase of such goods was the usual trade or business or whether it was an isolated event. This now casts doubt on the decision in *R&B Customs Brokers Ltd v UDT* (1988) where is was decided that in a case involving an exclusion clause, because the claimant buyer was a limited company and the car purchase for one of its directors was not an integral part of the business and was an isolated purchase, then that purchase was not made in the course of a business.

However, under the criminal law, where the burden of proof is higher, an isolated sale may not be in the course of a business. In *Davies v Sumner* (1984), a case under the Trade Descriptions Act 1968, the defendant was deemed not to be acting in the course of a business, when as a self-employed courier, he disposed of a car stating that the mileage was 20,000 when in fact it was 120,000 miles. Students are asked to note that this is a criminal statute and the defendant would have been subject to fines or imprisonment if he had been held to be acting in the course of a business. The words were given a much more restricted meaning than in *Stevenson v Rogers* where the case was being decided under section 14, and did not involve a criminal offence.

Goods have to be of satisfactory quality

Assuming that the seller is acting in the course of a business, section 14 says there is a condition that the goods must be of *satisfactory quality.* The Sale and Supply of Goods Act 1994 amended the old definition of merchantable quality so that all goods sold after January 3, 1995 have to conform to the new definition of satisfactory quality. The amendments made by the 2002 Regulations increase the liability of the retailer for public statements made about the goods.

What is satisfactory quality?

Satisfactory quality is defined in section 14(2A) and is expanded further in sections 14(2B) and 14(2D). Section 14(2A) says that goods are of satisfactory quality if they meet the standard that a reasonable person would regard as satisfactory, taking account of any description of the goods, the price (if relevant) and all other relevant circumstances.

Section 14(2B) says that the quality of goods includes their state and condition and the following (among others) are in appropriate cases aspects of the quality of goods:

(a) fitness for *all* the purposes for which the goods are supplied;
(b) appearance and finish;
(c) freedom from minor defects;
(d) safety; and
(e) durability.

In *Clegg v Olle Andersson* (2003) because the yacht was built with an overweight keel, which therefore affected the boat's safety, the yacht was deemed to be of unsatisfactory quality. In *Bacardi-Martini v Hardy* (2002) drinks contaminated with benzene were deemed to be of unsatisfactory quality. Clearly the drinks were not free from minor defects.

Section 14(2D) says that where the buyer deals as a consumer, the relevant circumstances described above in section 14(2A) include any public statements on the specific characteristics of the goods made by the seller, the producer or his representative particularly in advertising and labelling. This means that the seller may be liable for pre-publicity material claims made about the goods. If the product does not live up to claims on the labelling it may not be of satisfactory quality.

Below are some of the problems facing consumers in respect of defective goods.

1 What if they work but are dented and scratched?

2 What happens if the new goods can be easily repaired?
3 How does the section apply (if at all) to second hand goods?
4 What about the effect of manufacturers' guarantees?

The section will now be studied in detail to answer these questions, among others. The definition of satisfactory quality, which replaces merchantable quality, has taken into account some issues raised in problem areas and it is this definition which must be considered in relation to defective goods. However, as well as considering some recent satisfactory quality cases, some of the cases on *merchantable quality* will be considered below to illustrate that today these goods would also be deemed not to be of satisfactory quality.

As far as most consumers are concerned, if they pay a higher price they expect better quality and, as section 14(2A) states, price is a factor to be taken into consideration when deciding whether goods are of satisfactory quality or not. The old case of *Brown v Craiks* (1970) supports this view *i.e.* the more the consumer pays, the higher his quality expectations are. This is as true today in relation to satisfactory quality as it has been throughout all the old merchantable quality cases.

What about new goods? How long do we expect them to last for? The definition states durability is a factor but does not expand on this so it will have to be decided as a question of fact in each case. Several car cases decided under merchantable quality in recent years try to throw light on this particular question.

In *Bernstein v Pamson Motors* (1987), Mr Bernstein purchased a new Nissan car for cash. After three weeks and some 140 miles he was driving his car along the motorway when the engine "seized up". The reason for this was that a drop of sealant, which had got into the lubrication system when the car was being assembled, had caused a blockage that deprived the car of oil. In spite of a controversial judgment on other matters, Rougier J. held that the car was not of merchantable quality. A consumer who purchases a new car is entitled to expect that the engine will not seize up after three weeks. The car clearly would not be of satisfactory quality today.

What about appearance defects on new cars? In *Rogers v Parish* (1987), a new Range Rover car was purchased under a conditional sale agreement. On delivery there were defects in the engine, gearbox and bodywork and the oil seals were unsound. The claimant drove the car for some six months, constantly complained, but between visits to the garage managed to clock up 5,500 miles. At the end of six months, faults still remained in the gearbox, engine and bodywork.

On the question of the bodywork defects and the class of comfort to be expected interior-wise from a new car, the Court of Appeal said categorically that appearance defects in a new car can, depending on the price and standard expected, render a car to be of unmerchantable quality. This decision has now been given statutory force in that appearance defects for all goods, and not just cars, must be taken into account in deciding whether or not goods are of satisfactory quality. Consumers pay for their purchases to look good not just to perform a function.

The Court of Appeal decided in the *Parish* case again that the car was not of merchantable quality. Today again the goods would not be deemed to be of satisfactory quality. The Court of Appeal in the *Parish* case specifically tried to answer three questions that are of relevance to satisfactory quality.

(i) If the defect is repairable, does this mean that the car is of satisfactory quality? The answer given to this was no, so that if a consumer buys goods which would work perfectly if they were repaired, do they have to accept a repair? Clearly the answer is no. *Clegg v Olle Andersson* (2003). The definition states that the consumer is entitled to goods that are free from minor defects. However, from a practical point of view, if the seller is only prepared to repair and the consumer is unwilling to take the matter further, then this may be the only option available.

(ii) What about the effect of a manufacturer's warranty? If a consumer buys goods knowing that if they are defective they will be repaired free of charge under warranty, should the consumer anticipate defects and therefore the expectation of satisfactory quality is lower? This argument was rejected. It was stated very sensibly that a warranty could only increase expectations, it certainly could not diminish them.

(iii) The third argument, that the car could be driven, albeit intermittently between visits to the garage, was also rejected. The buyer had purchased a car for comfort, transportation and reliability. He was entitled to this constantly and not intermittently! As stated above, appearance defects now form part of the definition.

As far as consumers are concerned, most of the cases that are litigated tend to involve cars—being the most expensive product consumers usually purchase, and everyday items such as toasters, clothes etc., are either litigated through the Small Claims Court (see later) and the decisions are largely unreported, or else the consumer unfortunately decides the time and irritation involved are not worth it.

Are second hand goods covered?

Does the condition apply? The answer is yes, but obviously age and price are to be taken into account and the reasonable buyer's expectations. In *Bartlett v Sidney Marcus* (1965) the claimant purchased a second hand Jaguar for £950. He was told the clutch needed a small repair. However, when the car had been driven for 300 miles the car required a complete new clutch, costing £84. *Held*: the car was of merchantable quality, a clutch defect is the kind that could be anticipated in a secondhand car. The car would today be deemed to be of satisfactory quality. The point about Mr Bartlett knowing about the clutch will be discussed later.

In *Crowther v Shannon Motor Co.* (1975) again the car involved was a second hand Jaguar purchased for £390. This time the car, which had travelled 82,000 miles, was driven a further 2,500 miles in three weeks when the engine seized up. The Court of Appeal said this was a defect that could not reasonably be expected from a car of this age and mileage and there was a breach of merchantable quality. The car would today fail on the durability point and would not be of satisfactory quality.

In *Business Application Specialists v Nationwide Credit* (1988) the second hand car in question, a Mercedes, was purchased on hire purchase terms. The price was £14,850. After being driven for 800 miles the car broke down, suffering from loss of compression. The defect was likened to the clutch one in *Bartlett v Sidney Marcus* (1965) and the car was deemed to be of merchantable quality. Today the car would be of satisfactory quality.

In *Shine v General Guarantee* (1988) the car was a second hand Fiat X19, purchased on hire purchase terms for £4,400. The car had in fact been written off and disposed of for salvage purposes. The claimant discovered this after three months and sought to reject it. On the question of whether the car was of merchantable quality, the Court of Appeal said it was valid to take the buyer's expectations into account and ask what did the buyer think he was getting and what did he actually get?

As Bush J. said, what was the claimant entitled to think he was buying? He thought he was buying an enthusiast's car, a car of the mileage shown and at the sort of price cars of that age and condition could be expected to fetch. What he in fact was buying, was a car that had been submerged in water for at least 24 hours, and that was an insurance company write off. He was buying a potentially rogue car and irrespective of its condition, it was in fact one which no member of the public, knowing the facts, would touch with a barge pole unless they could get it at "a substantially reduced price to reflect the risk they were taking". The car was not of merchantable quality. Today the car would not be of satisfactory quality, it would not be fit for all the purposes for which goods of the kind in question are commonly supplied, *i.e.* it would have no second hand value.

Defects drawn to the buyer's attention

Section 14(2C)(a) says that goods must be of satisfactory quality unless the defect has been specifically drawn to the buyer's attention before the contract is made. Section 14(2C)(b) says that where the buyer has examined the goods there is no condition of satisfactory quality as regards defects that that examination ought to have revealed. It would therefore appear that it is much better to advise buyers not to examine goods before purchase. The buyer of a sweater who misses an obvious hole could be in danger of falling within this exception if he examined the goods before purchase and missed the hole. Note also *Bartlett v Sidney Marcus* (1965).

In *R&B Customs Brokers Ltd v UDT* (1988) the purchaser was aware of the fact that his second hand Colt Shogun had a leaky roof before the contract was concluded. (This was because the sale was made on a conditional sale agreement. The claimant managing director was allowed to take the car away before the finance company accepted him and therefore concluded the contract. For the mechanics of a conditional sale agreement, see p.52 below.) This defect could never be repaired. The Court of Appeal ruled there was no breach of section 14(2) as to merchantable quality because the claimant knew of the defect. This would be exactly the same today in relation to satisfactory quality.

All goods supplied are governed by the condition

Section 14 applies to *all* goods supplied under the contract so that if an extra is added *e.g.* as in *Wilson v Rickett Cockerell* (1954) (detonator in a bag of coalite) the defendant cannot argue that he supplied the goods and a detonator. The effect of the total package was to render the coalite unmerchantable and today not of satisfactory quality.

Strict liability and contractual liability

Section 14 creates "strict liability" *i.e.* it does not matter how careful the defendant is in checking his stock, if he sells defective goods he is liable: *Frost v Aylesbury Dairy* (1905).

Remember as well, section 14 creates contractual liability; it is the retailer who is liable under section 14 to the buyer. Making him liable for advertising and labelling claims has extended the retailer's liability. If the retailer chooses to join another party into the proceedings then he can do so, but he remains the one who is primarily liable. This is why it is vital from a retailer's point of view to have good indemnity clauses, reputable suppliers and good insurance cover.

Goods should be fit for their purpose

Section 14(3) of the Sale of Goods Act 1979 says that where the seller sells in the course of a business and the buyer *expressly* or by implication makes known any particular purpose for which the goods are being bought, there is an implied *condition* that the goods supplied are reasonably fit for that purpose except where the circumstances show that the buyer does not rely, or that it is unreasonable for him to rely, on the *skill or judgement of the seller*. It is a question of fact whether or not a product is fit for its purpose. In *Leicester Circuits Ltd v Coates* (2003), ink supplied for ink presses by the defendants to the claimants was ruled to be of satisfactory quality and fit for the buyers' purpose. It was ruled to be the buyers' fault when the ink caused problems, it had worked well for two years. The buyers could not show on the balance of probabilities that the ink was defective and unfit for its purpose. Expert evidence thought that the fault lay with the buyers' manufacturing process. In *Jewson Ltd v Kelly* (2003) boilers supplied by the claimants to the defendants were again ruled to be of satisfactory quality and fit for their purpose. Because of the specialist nature of the order, it was unfair for the buyers to claim a breach of section 14(3). They should have ensured the goods would match their needs and detailed specifications. It was unfair, ruled the Court of Appeal, to throw all responsibility onto the sellers so there was no breach of section 14(3) and the buyers had to pay for the goods.

One-purpose and multi-purpose goods

As consumers we frequently buy goods that only have one purpose. If a washing machine or a hot water bottle is purchased, then the buyer does not usually ask the sales assistant whether the machine will wash clothes or whether the bottle will keep them warm. The purpose is implied because they are one-purpose goods. Therefore, if the goods are defective there is a breach of section 14(2) and 14(3), *Priest v Last* (1903) (hole in hot water bottle). In the case of choosing goods, if the consumer goes to a reputable store, then he is entitled to assume that the seller has chosen his stock "using his skill" and therefore the requirement in section 14(3) is satisfied. *Grant v Australian Knitting Mills* (1936).

Supposing the buyer wishes to purchase a printer to accompany his computer. He visits a reputable store and asks for printer XZ 2000, not mentioning anything else to the retailer. It turns out that this printer is incompatible with his particular computer, but will work with many other brands. There is no breach of section 14(2) and no breach of section 14(3) as the buyer has not relied on the skill and judgement of the seller. When buying multi-purpose goods such as these, buyers should always be advised to ask as many questions as possible to get the maximum benefit under section 14(3). This was the case in *Griffiths v Peter Conway Ltd* (1939) where the buyer's skin was irritated by a fur coat purchased from the defendant. This would not have affected most buyers. There was no breach of section 14(2) or 14(3) as the fact the buyer had abnormally sensitive skin was never communicated to the seller. If the buyer of goods fails to make known that the goods are to be used for other than their normal purpose, then the extent of the seller's obligation is to ensure that the goods are fit for the purpose for which they would ordinarily be used. *Slater and Slater v Finning Ltd* (1996). Note: *Jewson Ltd v Kelly* (2003).

In *R&B Customs Brokers Ltd v UDT* (1988) (see above) the car had a leaky roof. There was no breach of merchantable quality at the time because of the proviso to section 14 that the buyer was aware of the defect. However, whenever it rained the car was impossible to use. When the buyer purchased the car he did not say to the salesman "I want to drive it in England and it rains in England. Will I be dry?" The car was not fit for its purpose of being driven in England and there was a breach of section 14(3).

3. REMEDIES IN SALE OF GOODS ACT CONTRACTS

The effect of the word "condition"

It has been seen so far that the terms in sections 13, 14(2) and 14(3) are all conditions. Their importance insofar as buyers are concerned is in relation to the remedies they can pursue. If there is a breach of condition, the buyer is entitled to reject the goods, recover any monies paid and is entitled to any further damages resulting as a natural and probable consequence of the breach.

This is of course the rule for remoteness of damage in the case of *Hadley v Baxendale* (1854).

Remedies for breach of contract in sale of goods contracts

As stated above, sections 13 and 14 are conditions normally entitling the buyer to reject the goods, however, section 11(4) of the Sale of Goods Act states "where a contract of sale is not severable and the buyer has *accepted* the goods, the breach of any condition is to be treated as a breach of warranty". The remedy for a breach of warranty is damages only, therefore, it is vital to know if acceptance has occurred for this can greatly affect the remedy.

What is acceptance?

The Sale and Supply of Goods Act 1994 has made a number of changes in favour of the buyer. Acceptance is governed by sections 34 and 35 of the Sale of Goods Act. It is section 35 that will be of most relevance to consumers. Section 35 says acceptance can occur in three ways.

(1) By intimation to the seller that he has accepted them. However section 35(2) states that where goods are delivered to the buyer and he has not previously examined

them, he is not deemed to have accepted them until he has had a reasonable opportunity of examining them to see if they conform to the terms of the contract. This right cannot be taken away from a consumer buyer so any consumer buyer who has signed a delivery note would not be deemed to have accepted goods until an examination has taken place whatever has been signed on the delivery note. Of course, it is still best advice to sign "received but not inspected" to avoid all problems.

(2) An act after delivery inconsistent with the seller's ownership. This is much more important in commercial rather than consumer cases.

(3) Retention beyond a reasonable time. This is the most important acceptance issue facing consumers, *i.e.* by the buyer retaining the goods beyond a reasonable time. If the buyer keeps the goods beyond a reasonable time he is deemed to have accepted them and is entitled to damages only. This is the most usual form of acceptance in consumer cases.

The questions to be asked therefore are:

(i) When does the time start to run?
(ii) What is considered reasonable?

As stated earlier, section 35 has been amended to take into account the case of *Bernstein v Pamson Motors* (1987). In this case, it will be recalled that Mr Bernstein had his car for three weeks when the engine seized up. The first time that Mr Bernstein knew anything was wrong was when his car blew up on the motorway. He was offered a replacement engine but wanted a new car or a refund. Rougier J. held, as stated earlier, that there was a breach of merchantable quality but that, by "keeping" the car for three weeks, Mr Bernstein had accepted the car and was entitled therefore to damages only, which meant in his case a replacement engine. Time ran from the moment of delivery not from when the defect occurred and three weeks, according to the judge, was too long to have had the car before rejecting it. Clearly, this case was not advantageous to consumers. The amendments mean that the law is now more favourable towards buyers.

Consumers must be given a reasonable opportunity to examine goods to see whether they conform to the contract

Like intimation acceptance, section 35(5) now states that in deciding whether a reasonable time has elapsed, the questions that should be asked include whether or not the buyer has had a reasonable opportunity of examining the goods to see that they conform to the contract. The word reasonable is mentioned many times. What is reasonable is a question of fact in every case and if a similar case to *Bernstein* occurred today, a judge would state that three weeks to test a new car is insufficient time to decide that it meets its contractual obligations. This is certainly the aim behind section 35(5). Therefore, acceptance would not have occurred and Mr Bernstein would be entitled to a refund. Note: *Michael Peakman v Express Circuits Ltd* (1998) where the buyer was not deemed to have accepted the goods after three weeks and was entitled to reject. More recently, in *Clegg v Olle Andersson* (2003), the Court of Appeal declared that the aim behind section 35(5) had been achieved, that the *Bernstein* case was wrong and that the buyer could reject his yacht after seven months. His initial complaint was made almost immediately after taking delivery and a period of negotiations and information seeking began. This information only reached the buyer some six months later. He rejected the yacht three weeks later. He was held not to have accepted the goods. The buyer had acted reasonably throughout and had not lost the right to reject. He had complained straightaway and having eventually received the information he required, he acted within three weeks, a reasonable time. To summarise, retaining the goods beyond a reasonable period of time still constitutes acceptance but reasonableness is a question of fact and the whole issue of reasonable opportunity to examine the goods must be considered.

Repairs and acceptance

The amending Sale and Supply of Goods Act 1994 has definitely cleared up one point on repairs. Merely by agreeing to a repair by the seller does not mean to say that the buyer has accepted the goods, section 35(6) of the Sale of Goods Act 1979. It used to be the case that by agreeing to a repair the consumer ran into acceptance problems.

The commercial unit

Under section 35(7) the concept of a commercial unit has been introduced. A commercial unit is defined as a unit, the division of which would materially impair the value of the goods or the character of the unit. If the buyer has accepted part of what is deemed to be a commercial unit his remedy will be confined to damages.

Note: problems on acceptance do not arise in hire purchase contracts or conditional sale agreements. This will be discussed further below. See p.23.

The best advice to be given to consumers therefore is to act quickly. However, recent amendments made in 2002 and discussed below will assist consumers further in this area.

Consumer buyers

From March 2003, where a buyer deals as a consumer, then the buyer has four additional remedies. A consumer is defined as a natural person, not a limited company, acting outside the purposes of his trade business or profession. Therefore, if John buys a lawnmower to cut the grass he is covered by the new remedies whereas Ian, the gardener, who attends to Bill's garden next door, cannot take advantage of these new remedies in respect of his lawnmower purchase. These new remedies are now contained in sections 48A to 48F of the Sale of Goods Act.

Where there has been any breach of the statutory implied terms as to description, satisfactory quality or fitness for purpose the extra four remedies are:

(1) the right to have the goods repaired;
(2) the right to have the goods replaced.

However, neither of these two remedies is available if it is either impossible or disproportionate to the original cost. The repair or replacement has to be carried out within a reasonable time and without significant inconvenience for the consumer. Once the buyer has agreed to one of these two remedies and the chosen remedy is provided within a reasonable time of being demanded, then the buyer is not given the option of either of the remaining two remedies.

The remaining two remedies are:

(3) rescission of the contract; or
(4) an appropriate reduction in the price *i.e.* a partial refund.

Remember that these extra two remedies are not available if the buyer has agreed to a repair or replacement and this has been offered by the seller.

These four extra remedy rights are entirely additional and do not take away any of the buyers old rights under the Sale of Goods Act as outlined earlier. They merely give extra rights to repair and replacement if this is the preferred choice of the buyer. However, once the buyer has chosen to ask the seller to repair or replace the goods under section 48, he must allow the seller a reasonable period of time to do so and he cannot during this time reject the goods. (Section 48D.) Equally, if the buyer agrees to a repair under section 48B and this is provided within a reasonable time and the goods are repaired so that they conform to the contract, then the buyer cannot reject the goods. Obviously, if the repair is unsuccessful, the buyer can pursue other remedies.

The burden of proof in relation to these additional four remedies is more favourable towards the buyer. Section 48 of the Sale of Goods Act states these remedies are available where goods do not conform to the contract. Goods do not conform when they are misdescribed, are of unsatisfactory quality or are unfit for their purpose. If this happens during the first six months after delivery, then section 48A creates a presumption that the goods were non-conforming when they were delivered. In other words, if goods "fail" within six months, then the presumption is that they were defective from the outset and the consumer is entitled to exercise his rights to these four additional remedies.

OTHER REMEDIES ISSUES

Rejection for minor breaches of condition

The law of contract is such that any breach of contract can give rise to a right to reject the goods and obtain a full refund. THIS IS THE CASE WHERE THE BUYER DEALS AS A CONSUMER SUBJECT TO THE ACCEPTANCE DOCTRINE, as set out above. Thus, for example, if there is the smallest breach of description the consumer buyer can reject the goods provided he has not accepted them. The consumer buyer is of course now able to exercise his rights to the four extra remedies set out above.

What happens to a business buyer?

The amending 1994 Act has now drawn a distinction between a consumer buyer and a business buyer in relation to the remedy obtainable for a minor breach. Section 15A of the Sale of Goods Act states that where the buyer is not a consumer and the breach is so slight that it would be unreasonable for him to reject, the breach is to be treated as a breach of warranty. However, section 15A applies only to certain breaches of contract, *i.e.* breaches of sections 13 and 14 of the Sale of Goods Act 1979 relating to description, satisfactory quality and fitness for purpose. So, for example, if a business orders 100 components and say 3 are defective, then this will be a minor breach of section 14 as to satisfactory quality. The buyer would be limited to a damages only remedy in respect of the three defective components.

The wrong quantity delivered

Section 30(2A) of the 1979 Act also applies the same reasoning in relation to delivery of the wrong quantity to a business buyer. Again, if the buyer receives more or less than he contracted to buy, and the shortfall or excess is very slight then, although there is a breach of contract, it will be treated as a breach of warranty.

Who has to show that it is a minor breach?

For both sections 15A and 30(2A) the onus is on the seller to show that the breach, shortfall or excess, is slight, sections 15A(3) and 30(2B). So in the example given above where 3 out of 100 components were defective, it would be up to the seller to show that this breach is a minor one. Business buyers of course are not given the benefit of the additional remedies as these only apply to consumer buyers.

The right of partial rejection

By section 35A of the 1979 Act, a new right of partial rejection has been given to both business and consumer buyers. The Act now gives a right of partial rejection in certain circumstances where a buyer chooses to retain part of the goods and reject the remainder of the consignment. By deciding to accept part, the buyer does not lose his right to reject the remainder. For example, supposing a buyer has ordered 24 bottles of wine, 24 are delivered but 10 do not match the description ordered. The buyer can choose to keep the 14 bottles and reject the 10 incorrect ones.

The measure of damages

If the buyer has not accepted the goods, he will be entitled to reject the goods and claim any consequential losses. If he has accepted, then damages is the only remedy. The consumer buyer can of course elect one of the four additional remedies. As a Sale of Goods Act transaction is only a contract then, as stated earlier, the rules for the payment of damages are based on the case of *Hadley v Baxendale* (1854). Sections 51 to 53 of the Sale of Goods Act set out in more detail the kind of damages that can be claimed and how a figure can be reached, but it is important that students remember that what they are considering is the rule in *Hadley v Baxendale* (1854).

For example, suppose George purchases a kettle. After two weeks the kettle explodes, injuring George who is standing nearby, and ruining George's floor covering and kitchen units. George is entitled, under the Sale of Goods Act, to claim a breach of section 14 as to satisfactory quality. Assuming that he has not accepted the goods, he can claim a refund for the product from the retailer. He could of course claim a replacement if he so desired. As his personal injuries and property damage resulted from the breach he is entitled to claim damages for these losses based on the rule in *Hadley v Baxendale* (1854).

For the next example let us suppose George purchased a music system nine months ago which has "chewed up" four cassettes costing £30. Because of the time factor, George will almost certainly have accepted the goods and will be unable to reject. He could choose a repair or replacement option as he has the four extra remedies but, as more than six months has elapsed, the burden of proof will be on George to show that the goods were defective from the outset. Most retailers will offer a repair unless this is disproportionate to the cost of the goods (replacement may be cheaper) and this is the remedy George will have to agree to. He will be entitled to damages for breach of warranty for the product (see section 53). In this case it will be the cost of putting the unit right. Repair is therefore the most likely outcome in this case. He will also be entitled to claim the cost of the four cassettes under the rule in *Hadley v Baxendale* (1854).

Other damages issues

Other issues that face consumers are:

(a) Even if they can obtain a refund for defective goods, they may have to pay more for the same goods elsewhere. These additional costs arise as a result of the natural and probable consequences of the breach and can be reclaimed.
(b) The seller is unable to deliver the goods on time.

Suppose George orders a bed for £300 with delivery to take place on Friday. If the bed is not delivered George has suffered a breach of contract but unless he made "time of the essence" he is not entitled to regard the contract as "terminated": *Rickards v Oppenheim* (1950). He is entitled to damages (if he can prove loss) but will have to give the retailer another chance to deliver. If the retailer fails to deliver this time and George is put to extra costs buying the goods elsewhere he can claim these additional costs.

There is now a replacement remedy under the Sale of Goods Act

It should be noted that there is now a replacement remedy provided in the Sale of Goods Act. This is contained in section 48B of Sale of Goods Act. Advice should be taken as to the remedy sought. Remember, this must not be disproportionate to the original cost of the goods.

Damages for distress and disappointment

This is a head of damages that should not be overlooked in consumer cases despite the reluctance of the Court of Appeal in the case of *Hayes v Dodd* (1990) to extend this kind of award. Damages for distress have been awarded in holiday cases, for loss of photographs, and in one instance where the bride's wedding carriage failed to turn up. However, in the case of *Alexander v Rolls Royce* (1995) the Court of Appeal said that breach of a contract to repair a Rolls Royce properly did not give rise to liability for damages for distress and disappointment. The Court was therefore following the *Hayes v Dodd* line.

Actions involving guarantees

Actions discussed so far have involved a claim in contract against the seller. Regulation 15 of the Sale and Supply of Goods to Consumers Regulations 2002 provides that where goods are sold or otherwise supplied to a consumer, which are offered with a consumer guarantee, the consumer guarantee takes effect as a contractual obligation. This now means that a consumer will be able to enforce rights against a manufacturer direct when a manufacturer promises such rights and remedies in a guarantee. Previously of course, a consumer would have been faced with privity of contract problems. This is a good step forward for consumers.

4.   OTHER CONSUMER TRANSACTIONS

In the previous chapters, transactions covered by the Sale of Goods Act have been considered. However, there are many transactions consumer buyers make and, because there is no "transfer of property for a monetary consideration called the price", the transaction is not governed by the Sale of Goods Act.

It has been seen that if Ben buys a car for cash, then if the car turns out to be defective, Ben has a remedy under the Sale of Goods Act.

Hire purchase transactions

However, what is the position if Ben decided to buy his car on hire purchase terms? (The mechanics of this are discussed later.) In this case there is merely a "bailment of goods". The finance company owns the goods until the final instalment is paid so there is no transfer of property. The car is defective. What can Ben do?

This hire purchase consumer transaction is governed by the Supply of Goods (Implied Terms) Act 1973. Sections 9 and 10 of this Act mirror exactly the provisions of sections 13 and 14 of the Sale of Goods Act (a great sigh of relief from all students and practitioners at this point as there are no new provisions to be learnt) so that if the car is defective there will be a breach of section 10 of the Act as to satisfactory quality and fitness for purpose. All the student has to realise is that, where a hire purchase transaction is involved, section 10 of the 1973 Act must be considered instead of section 14 of the 1979 Act.

Differences in approach

There is, however, one major difference between hire purchase defective goods transactions and straight sale of goods transactions and this involves the issue of acceptance. Students will recall that sale of goods transactions are caught by section 11(4) of the Sale of Goods Act, which has the effect of turning a condition into a warranty if acceptance has occurred. There is no equivalent provision in the 1973 Act so no issue of acceptance arises, only the common law doctrine of affirmation.

Affirmation v acceptance

Affirmation is more favourable to consumer buyers as it can only occur when the defect is known and time starts to run from that point. In *Shine v General Guarantee* (1988), involving a hire purchase transaction, it was held that by his actions the buyer had affirmed the contract (he had been slow to reject the goods). Therefore, he was entitled to damages only.

However, in *Farnworth Finance Facilities v Attryde* (1970), the goods in question was a motorbike. Some four months and 400 miles later, Mr Attryde attempted to reject the goods. *Held:* he was entitled to do so. As Lord Denning said "A man only affirms a contract when he knows of the defects and by his conduct elects to go on with the contract despite them". Again in *Yeoman Credit v Apps* (1962) the buyer had the use of the motorbike for some time and was entitled to reject it and recover nearly all monies paid. A small allowance for use was made. It should be noted that in relation to remedies no amendment has been made to the 1973 Act creating the four additional remedies enjoyed by consumers buying under a Sale of Goods Act 1979 contract. Affirmation therefore still remains very important in hire purchase transactions.

Conditional sale transactions

This type of credit transaction is covered by the Sale of Goods Act as it is a sale subject to a condition. However, in the Supply of Goods (Implied Terms) Act 1973 it is enacted that section 11(4) does not apply to these transactions. The doctrine of acceptance does not apply again, only affirmation.

In *Rogers v Parish (Scarborough) Ltd* (1987) the buyer of a new Range Rover under a conditional sale agreement had the goods for six months, driving 5,000 miles with constant complaints and return visits to the garage. *Held:* he had not affirmed the contract and was entitled to a refund. Buyers in a conditional sale agreement have the benefit of the four additional remedies as this is governed by Sale of Goods Act.

Hire transactions

These are governed by Supply of Goods and Services Act 1982. Sections 8 and 9 are the equivalents of sections 13 and 14 of the Sale of Goods Act so that if Ben hires a car and it is defective, he has to seek a remedy under this statute.

Exchange transactions

If there is a pure exchange transaction, involving no extra cash, then there is no monetary consideration. (See *Esso Petroleum v Customs and Excise Commissioners* (1976)—World Cup coins 1966 promotion—where the consideration was not cash but buying of four gallons of petrol.) Therefore, the transaction is not governed by the Sale of Goods Act. So if Ben swaps his Mercedes for a Mini, the transaction is not governed by the Sale of Goods Act but is instead again governed by Part I of the Supply of Goods and Services Act. This time sections 3 and 4 apply. These are the equivalents of sections 13 and 14 of the Sale of Goods Act. Again, the doctrine of affirmation applies.

If, however, any additional cash is paid over with the exchange goods, then the transaction is back under the Sale of Goods Act. Therefore, if Ben hands over his car together with £1,000 to acquire his new one, the Sale of Goods Act governs the transaction.

The materials part of a work and materials contract

Ben takes his car to be serviced. As a consumer he is paying for the work to be completed to his satisfaction but the supplier will also be using parts in the course of the services. It is liability for those parts, in the event that they are defective, or do not match their description, which is now being considered.

Liability for parts supplied under a work and materials contract is governed again by sections 3 and 4 of Part I of the Supply of Goods and Services Act (the equivalents of sections 13 and 14). Again, the doctrine of affirmation applies. Therefore, if Ben's car is supposed to be fitted with genuine "Vord" parts and fake "Boda" parts have been used, Ben will use this statute to pursue his action. In respect of exchange goods and the materials part of a work and materials contract, the buyer has the benefit of the four extra additional remedies.

The service part of a work and materials contract and pure service contract

In the example given above, of Ben taking his car to have it serviced, it is the service part of the contract that is now being considered.

In every work and materials contract and every pure service contract there is an implied term under section 13 of the Supply of Goods and Services Act that the work will be carried out with reasonable care and skill. Notice the difference between liability for failure to perform the work properly and liability for defective materials. The work has to be carried out with *reasonable* care and skill. The standard by which this can be judged is therefore an *objective negligence-based* standard as set in the famous case of *Bolam v Friern Hospital* (1957), a case involving the medical profession whereby to decide whether a doctor is liable for negligence, he must be compared with the average doctor in the profession.

Ben therefore would have to show, if he is complaining about the work, that the average garage mechanic would have performed the work differently. This is the case in all matters involving services whether it is a garage, a decorator or a plumber for example, where the quality of the services rendered is claimed to be unsatisfactory. The 2002 Regulations have amended the 1982 Act in one important area. Previously a buyer would have to be content with a damages-only remedy in respect of poor workmanship but in the case of a work and materials contract involving installation, the buyer now has available the four additional remedies. These are offered to a consumer not only where there is a breach of one of the terms relating to description, satisfactory quality, fitness for purpose and sample but also if the sale contract involves installation and this has been badly done, (section 11S of Supply of Goods and Services Act 1982). For example, a consumer can now elect in the case of a bad kitchen installation where the supplier has supplied and fitted the units to have the trader refit the units.

Reasonable time and payment terms

Two other terms are implied into service contracts. By section 14 of the Supply of Goods and Services Act where no time has been agreed for performing the contract, the supplier must perform it within a reasonable time.

By section 15 of the Supply of Goods and Services Act where no price has been agreed, then a reasonable price must be charged. If the supplier has quoted a very high price and this has been accepted by the consumer, then section 15 will not help him. He has entered into a bad bargain.

Remedies for breach of service contracts

The normal remedy for a breach of service contract is damages to put the poor work right and to restore the aggrieved consumer to the position he would have been in, had the contract been performed properly. However, note the availability of the four additional remedies where the service complained of is bad installation in a work and materials contract.

Damages for distress, disappointment and inconvenience have been frequently awarded for breach of service contracts despite the restrictive approach in *Hayes v Dodd* (1990). Holidays are a particular area that remain unaffected by this decision, *e.g. Jarvis v Swan Tours* (1973) as are "lost" photographs, *e.g. Woodman v Photo Trade Processing* (1981).

---

5. PRODUCT LIABILITY

It has already been noted in earlier chapters that where a buyer of goods is injured as a result of the product being defective, then he can recover for his personal injuries by "latching" them onto a claim that the goods are not of satisfactory quality and that the natural and probable consequence of that breach is that an injury occurred, *i.e.* the normal contractual rule for damages as set out in *Hadley v Baxendale* (1854).

This remedy is satisfactory of course, provided the person has actually purchased the goods and therefore has a contract under the Sale of Goods Act or that the supplier is still in existence. However, what happens if the person injured was given the defective product or a third party is injured by it? (Where the product is merely defective but has not caused damage, then students should note the possibility in some situations of using the Contracts (Rights of Third Parties) Act 1999. This confers the benefit of contractual rights on named third parties, thus attempting to find a way around the privity of contract rule. Directly enforceable rights are available against manufacturers, as widened by the Sale and Supply of Goods to Consumers Regulations 2002.)

However, in respect of injuries caused by defective products involving claims against the manufacturer, the most important statute to employ is the Consumer Protection Act 1987.

Prior to 1987, an injured person pursuing a claim against a manufacturer would have had to use the tort of negligence and the case of *Donoghue v Stevenson* (1932). The difficulties of proving fault, even though a duty of care is owed to the ultimate consumer, meant the consumer faced an uphill battle at times (*Daniels & Daniels v R White & Sons & Tarbard* (1938)).

Faced with these difficulties, and in an attempt to standardise product liability throughout Europe, the Consumer Protection Act was enacted in 1987.

SOME GENERAL POINTS

(a) The term product liability means that the person injured by defective products may have the right to sue for damages. Product liability is the term given to laws affecting those rights.

(b) The rights set out earlier under the Sale of Goods Act and in the tort of negligence are in addition to the rights given out in the Consumer Protection Act. The Act does not affect any existing civil laws governing product liability.

(c) The Act implements the European Communities Directive on Product Liability (85/374).

(d) The Act is NOT retrospective. It only affects products first supplied after March 1, 1988.

THE AIMS OF THE ACT

The major aims of the Act are to impose *strict liability* for defective products, principally on someone who is deemed to be a producer of the product, thus removing the requirement of having to prove fault. In *Abouzaid v Mothercare (UK) Ltd* (2000), the claimant failed in negligence but succeeded using the Act. The Act seeks to provide a clear route by which an injured person can reach the person responsible for the damage.

Basic position

Remember, the Act only applies where the consumer has a defective product that causes damage.

Section 2(1) of the Act says where any damage is caused wholly or partly by a defect in a product, every person to whom subsection (2) applies shall be liable for the damage. Therefore, the essential elements are:

(1) a product;
(2) damage;
(3) defective (in the way of being unsafe);
(4) causation;
(5) who is liable?

Who is liable?

As can be seen at the outset, there is no fault-based requirement. The Act is aimed at the person who was responsible for the product, not the person who supplied it. Therefore, the first consideration is who is liable? Section 2(2) says the following persons are primarily liable:

(a) the producer, *i.e.* the manufacturer;
(b) an own brander who has held himself out as a producer; and
(c) the first importer into the European Community.

The main purpose is to provide a clear route for the injured person to sue. Strict liability will attach to anyone who presents themselves as a producer, *e.g.* Sony, Philips, Hoover, or to anyone who is an own brander who has held himself out to be a producer of the product, *e.g.* Tesco, Marks & Spencer, Asda. It remains to be seen through case law whether a phrase like "produced for Tesco" will be judged to mean that Tesco are not liable under section 2(2) or whether they will only escape liability by actually naming the manufacturer, *i.e.* "made for J. Sainsbury by Fred Bloggs & Co."

The first importer into the European Community is also primarily liable so that if a Japanese television set is imported into France then transported to England where it causes damage to an individual, then the French importer is liable but not the British importer under the Act.

The position of the supplier

Only in relatively few cases will the supplier be liable. This is where the producer cannot be identified and the supplier is unable to identify anyone further up the chain of supply within a reasonable period of time. Suppliers of products must therefore ensure that they keep records of all companies who supply them with goods so that if a claim is made they will be able to pass this information onto the injured person. Even if their supplier has gone into liquidation, the person who actually supplied the goods will have fulfilled their obligations under the Consumer Protection Act by giving a name.

[**Note:** however, if the injured person actually bought the goods, there would be liability under the Sale of Goods Act by virtue of the contractual situation and no escape for the supplier.]

Main and component manufacturers

It should be further noted that some products are comprised of a number of different component items. In that case, the manufacturer of the total finished product is liable, *e.g.* a car manufacturer such as Ford, as is the manufacturer of the defective component concerned. Let us say the defective product is a tyre manufactured by Dunlop. The injured person can sue either the manufacturer of the total finished product or the component manufacturer or both, as liability is joint and several. So, for example, if a person is injured in circumstances as outlined above, both Ford and Dunlop could be drawn into an action.

What is a product?

By section 1(2) a product includes goods or electricity and this is further expanded by the definition in section 45, which states that goods includes growing crops and things comprised in land by virtue of being attached to it and any ship, aircraft or vehicle. The Consumer Protection Act 1987 (Product Liability) (Modification) Order 2000 makes unprocessed agricultural products, products for the purposes of the Act. Prior to the modification order, agricultural products such as cattle and sheep, for example, had to undergo an industrial process before qualifying as a product. It is extremely unlikely in the context of an examination question that a problem will be set where the student has to worry about whether the product is covered by the product definition under the Act. Blood and blood products are products covered by the Act. *A and Ors v National Blood Authority* (2001).

What is a defective product?

This is governed by section 3 which states that a defective product is defined as one where the *safety* of the product is not such as persons generally are entitled to expect. A product will not be considered defective simply because it is of poor quality or because a safer version is subsequently put on the market. Defects are likely to fall into three areas:

(a) MANUFACTURING: these should be the easiest to deal with in practice, *e.g.* the hot water bottle that splits because defective rubber has been used;

(b) DESIGN: this is going to present more difficulties in practice; or

(c) MISLEADING WARNING NOTICES: that fail to advise the consumer how to use the product properly, or no warning notices at all where a court might feel that a warning should have been given. There are, for example, product liability cases in America where no warnings were placed on a bottle of perfume. When the user stood up in front of a fire and caught fire, she argued that a warning should have been placed on the bottle pointing out that the contents were flammable and telling the user not to stand in front of fires. This led to a successful claim. However, the claim based on misleading warning notices failed in the case of *Worsley v Tambrands Ltd* (1999).

On a question of causation, the claimant must show that the defect caused the damage. Cases in tort, such as *Wilsher v Essex Area Health Authority* (1986), *Kay v Ayrshire* (1982) will no doubt be used in this area where difficult cases arise.

What kind of damage is covered?

It is important to note that only certain kinds of damage are covered by the Act and therefore at the outset, if the kind of damage that does occur is not within section 5 of the Act, it is pointless pursuing a claim and redress under the Sale of Goods Act or negligence must be sought.

A person can sue under the Act (section 5) for:

(a) death;
(b) personal injury; or
(c) damage to private property valued above £275.

There is no liability for damage to the product itself or for the loss of, or any damage to, the whole or any part of any product that has been supplied with the product. Thus, if Fred buys a new car and one of the tyres is defective due to a manufacturing defect and Fred has a crash in the car, causing personal injuries and the car is considered to be a "write off", Fred can sue for his personal injury under the Act but cannot sue for the car. He CANNOT argue that the tyre and the chassis are different products thus the tyre has caused damage to other property (as was tried in *Aswan Engineering Establishment Co. v Lupdine Ltd* (1987)). The car was acquired AT ONE TIME, thus any compensation for the car itself must be achieved via the Sale of Goods Act. If Fred, however, replaced the tyres on his car, and the new tyres were defective, this time he COULD claim compensation for his injuries *and* his car as one product, the tyre, has caused damage to another product, the car. This of course assumes the car is private property.

Section 5(3) attempts to define private property by saying:

A person shall not be liable under section 2 for damage to property that is not:

(a) of a description ordinarily intended for private use, occupation or consumption; and
(b) intended by the person suffering the loss mainly for his own private use occupation or consumption. It will be a question of fact whether the property is private and

difficulties will arise in "office equipment at home" and "personal items in the office". Remember: the property damage must be valued at more than £275. This is to discourage frivolous claims under the Act.

Defences

Even if a manufacturer is liable so far under the Act, the Act creates strict liability not absolute liability and in the United Kingdom we have opted to give manufacturers six defences. The burden of proof rests on the defendant.

The defences are:

(1) The defect was caused by complying with the law. The defence is only available where the standard is a mandatory one. It will not help a producer where compliance with a standard is only advisory, as is the case with many products conforming to British Standard. The producer must show that the defect was the inevitable consequence of complying with the standard. Needless to say, this is unlikely to prove to be a much-used defence in practice!

(2) That he did not supply the product—this covers cases, for instance, of theft. A further definition of the word "supply" can be found in section 46.

(3) That the supplier is not in business. The aim behind the Act is to impose strict liability on commercial producers and it was never the intention to impose liability on private individuals. However, section 4(1)(c) is worded in such a way that private individuals may be caught, it says:

    (a) that where the only supply of the product to another by the person proceeded against was otherwise than in the course of a business;

AND

    (b) that the supplier is not a producer, then there is a defence under the Act. Therefore, sales of second hand goods by private individuals are not caught by the Act. However if the supplier is a producer and he did make the goods with a view to profit, then even though he is a private individual, he will be caught by the Act.

Thus, a grandfather who makes a toy for his grandson is a producer but is not doing it with a view to profit so is not caught by the Act. A housewife who makes home-made jam for a local church charity bazaar should not be liable. But, a housewife on a busy coastal route who sells her home-made strawberry jam to passers-by from her front garden, would be liable.

(4) That the defect did not exist in the product at the time it was supplied by the producer to another. Examples involving the spiking of baby food serve to illustrate the point. If the food left the factory in perfect condition and the contamination took place in the supermarket, the manufacturer would not be liable. If the contamination occurred in the factory, the manufacturer would be liable. Of course, if the contamination took place in the supermarket the retailer would incur liability under the Sale of Goods Act for a breach of section 14 of the Sale of Goods Act.

(5) The state of scientific and technical knowledge at the relevant time was not such that a producer of products of the same description as the product in question might be expected to have discovered the defect.

This is the most controversial defence provided in the Act, "the state of the art defence". It has been condemned by many commentators as giving producers a "get out" under the Act and in many cases where the Act could have proved to be most useful, *e.g.* in a similar scenario like the thalidomide drug case, the manufacturer may still escape liability.

In order to avail themselves of the defence, producers will have to show that at the relevant time they could not have been expected to discover the defect. In the House of Lords debate H.L. Vol. 483, ser. 25, col. 841, it was said:

> "It will be of no help to the producer to plead how difficult or how expensive it had or might have been to have found the answers to that defect. If other producers of products of that type had the knowledge available to them, then the defence is of no use to the producer of the product".

The test under the Act is an objective one, not what the actual defendant knew, but what was actually known at the time. The defence failed in the case of *Abouzaid v Mothercare(UK) Ltd* (2000). In 1997 the European Commission failed in an attempt to show that the United Kingdom had drafted this defence too widely and that it should be amended.

(6) That a producer of a component produced a defective product and the defect was wholly attributable to instructions he had been given by the principal producer. This is a defence only open to a component manufacturer who has produced goods to a certain specification and the principal product is defective. The component manufacturer may be able to escape liability although the principal manufacturer could not. Thus if Bloggs Ltd supplies a component to Classit Ltd and the component makes the product defective because Classit's designs are faulty and Bloggs complied with all Classit's requirements, Bloggs would have a defence under the Act.

When must a claim be brought?

There are two matters to note here:

(1) In respect of personal injuries or property damage, the injured individual has three years in which to start a claim. Schedule 1, paragraph 1, amending Limitation Act 1980.
(2) As far as the manufacturer is concerned, there is a 10-year cut-off point from the time he supplied the product to the retailer. Manufacturers will therefore have to keep good records of all their transactions.

From a practical point of view, insurance is going to assume a much greater importance in this area, as are well drafted indemnity clauses between persons in the distribution chain.

RECALL NOTICES

Rarely a day goes by without seeing a recall notice for a product in a local or national newspaper. A recall notice cannot relieve a manufacturer of liability under the Act, he has still produced a defective product. However, there can be a reduction in damages on the grounds of contributory negligence if the consumer carried on using the product when he was aware of the recall.

6. EXCLUSION NOTICES

As has been seen, the Sale of Goods Act, the Supply of Goods (Implied Terms) Act, and the Supply of Goods and Services Act, give the buyer many rights in terms of description, satisfactory quality, fitness for purpose and the kind of service that can be expected.

What is the effect if the seller or the supplier attempts to escape his obligations, *i.e.* to exclude liability? What if the shopper is confronted with notices such as:

(a) "once the goods have left the store we accept no responsibility for them";
(b) "no refunds";
(c) "no returns"; or
(d) "unless you return goods within 48 hours we will not entertain any complaints about the goods we sell".

When taking a film to be developed, consumers are often met with a standard clause stating:

> "In the event of loss, our liability is limited to the cost of a replacement film".

When walking in a store car park, the customer often sees notices such as:

> "We accept no responsibility for damage or injuries caused to consumers using this car park howsoever caused".

It can be seen that the effect of all of these clauses is that someone is trying to escape liability.

Can this be done?

First, the starting point for all exclusion clauses is to see whether or not they have been INCORPORATED INTO the contract, for if incorporation has not occurred the clauses have no effect.

INCORPORATION

The common law rules as to incorporation must be considered.

(1) If consumers sign a document then the clause is incorporated, in the absence of:
  (a) misrepresentation—*Curtis v Chemical Cleaning Co.* (1951) 1 K.B. 805;
  (b) the *non est factum* rule.

  The basic rule therefore is that once consumers have signed, incorporation takes place and consumers are bound by the terms subject to the Unfair Contract Terms Act and the Unfair Terms in Consumer Contract Regulations 1999.

(2) (a) If the term is contained in an unsigned document, *e.g.* contained on a ticket or notice, the terms will only form part of the contract if reasonable steps were taken to bring it to the notice of the other party before the contract is made.

  (b) In an unsigned document, if the term is particularly onerous or unusual, it must be drawn to the other party's attention otherwise the term will not be incorporated. *Interfoto Picture Library v Stiletto* (1988). Here, the defendants found themselves with a bill for almost £4,000 when they retained some transparencies beyond a stated date. Unknown to them, the cost of keeping them beyond the date was £5.00 plus VAT per slide per day and as nearly 50 slides were involved, the bill totalled almost £4,000. The Court of Appeal held this onerous term had never been incorporated and the defendants could pay on a *quantum meruit* basis.

(3) The type of document involved, *e.g.* the famous deck chair case of *Chapelton v Barry UDC* (1940) will be considered. Here, a receipt could not be expected to contain vitally important exclusion clauses. There was no incorporation.

(4) Sometimes exclusion clauses that, for a first time consumer might not be incorporated into a contract, could be incorporated by a course of dealings. See dicta in *Spurling v Bradshaw* (1956), *McCutcheon v David MacBrayne* (1964). Students should therefore watch out for questions such as: "Joe has purchased furniture from Sell it Fast on a number of occasions. Each time, after he has paid, he was given a piece of paper with much small print. He never bothered reading it and always threw it away as he left the store". There is a possibility in answering a question like this, subject to what has been said above, that the

clause could have been incorporated by a course of dealings.

(5) Does the clause cover the event that has occurred? Students should remember their contract law and doctrines, such as the *contra preferentem* rule. However, since the advent of the Unfair Contract Terms Act 1977, the courts seem to have placed less importance on these older doctrines and more on the construction of the Act.

(6) Unless students are given a choice, "a two-tier" question, where they can answer one part as if incorporation has occurred and one part where it has not, then the question should always be answered on the basis that incorporation has occurred. Marks are bound to have been allocated for a discussion of the Unfair Contract Terms Act and the Unfair Terms in Consumer Contracts Regulations 1999 and students who opt for non-incorporation will only lose out.

Exclusion clauses are now governed by two sets of legislation, the Unfair Contract Terms Act 1977 as amended by 2002 Sale and Supply of Goods to Consumers Regulations and the Unfair Terms in Consumer Contracts Regulations 1999. These will now be considered in turn.

THE UNFAIR CONTRACT TERMS ACT 1977

Points to Note

(1) The Unfair Contract Terms Act, where it operates:
   (a) has the effect of making certain exclusion clauses void;
   (b) has the effect of making certain clauses subject to the reasonableness test.

(2) The Act governs any clause that purports to restrict or avoid liability. Section 13 of the Unfair Contract Terms Act.

(3) The Act does not *create* new duties; it merely controls clauses that cut down a duty.

(4) The major provisions of the Act (sections 2 to 7), with the exception of section 6, only apply to business liability. Section 1(3) of the UCTA. The Act is primarily designed to "get at" businesses that are trying to exclude liability, not at private individuals.

(5) Schedule 1 to the Act contains a number of cases where the Act will not apply. The most important are contracts of insurance and any contract relating to the creation, transfer or termination of an interest in land.

Where does the Act operate?

So far as examinations are concerned, and in practice, the Act operates in *three major areas:*

(1) Where exclusions in relation to the implied terms sections 13 and 14 of the Sale of Goods Act 1979 (and their equivalents in the Supply of Goods (Implied Terms) Act 1973 and the Supply of Goods and Services Act 1982) are concerned, *e.g.* "once the goods have left the store, we take no responsibility for them". "No refunds under any circumstances."

(2) The person supplying the goods or services is trying to exclude their negligence-based liability. Remember that section 13 of the Supply of Goods and Services Act says a service has to be supplied with reasonable care and skill. If a trader tries to exclude liability for the way in which the work has been performed, he is trying to exclude his negligence-based liability, *e.g.* a garage has a notice that states: "once the cars have left our premises any accidents are the responsibility of the customer. We accept no liability".

(3) The person supplying the goods or services is trying to exclude liability for any other breach of contract, *e.g.* a clause in a removal contract limiting liability for breakages to £40 per item or for delay to £100.

The implied terms

Any attempt to exclude liability for a breach of the implied terms in sections 13 and 14 is void *where the buyer is dealing as a consumer*. Section 6 of the UCTA.

What is dealing as a consumer?

Section 12 of the Unfair Contract Terms Act as amended by 2002 Regulations defines dealing as a consumer as:

"a party deals as a consumer if he/she is an individual and

(a) he neither makes the contract in the course of a business nor holds himself out as doing so; and

(b) the other party does make the contract in the course of a business."

Therefore, if Joanna, a private individual, purchases a washing machine from Bewis's, a discount store, Joanna is dealing as a consumer. If, when she purchased the machine, she signed an invoice that stated no refunds given under any circumstances, this is clearly an attempt to exclude liability for satisfactory quality, *i.e.* section 14 of the Sale of Goods Act. Joanna satisfies the definition of dealing as a consumer, therefore the clause is void and Joanna can sue for a breach of satisfactory quality. Changes have also been made to Section 12(2) concerning auction sales and the status of buyers at these events.

Points to Note

(1) The onus is on the retailer to show that the other party to the contract is dealing as a non-consumer, section 12(3). So, in the example given above, the burden of proof is on Bewis's to show that Joanna is a non-consumer.

(2) In the light of the amendments made by the 2002 Regulations, the Court of Appeal decision in *R&B Customs Brokers Ltd v UDT* (1988) is probably incorrect. Here the claimant limited company were held to be dealing as consumers when they purchased a car for the use of the managing director. Although the regulations do not affect a limited company buyer as they are not individuals and consumers, a court would surely nowadays declare that the buyers were acting in the course of a business. That would mean they were dealing as non-consumers and any exclusion clauses regarding fitness for purpose would not be struck out as being void.

(3) If it is a hire purchase transaction then once again if the buyer deals as a consumer the equivalents of sections 13 and 14 in the 1973 Supply of Goods (Implied Terms) Act, *i.e.* sections 9 and 10 can never be excluded. Again, this is section 6 of the UCTA.

Where the buyer deals as a non-consumer, a clause excluding the implied terms under sections 13 and 14 of the Sale of Goods Act is subject to the reasonableness test. This would now be the case in *R&B Customs Brokers Ltd v UDT* outlined earlier.

The reasonableness test under the Unfair Contract Terms Act

Schedule 2 to the Unfair Contract Terms Act lays down a *non-exhaustive* list of guidelines, these include:

(a) the strength of the bargaining position between the parties;
(b) whether the customer received any inducement to agree to the term;
(c) whether the customer knew of the term; and
(d) whether the goods were specially manufactured.

Again, the onus of proving the clause is reasonable lies on the party seeking to rely upon it.

The following cases serve to illustrate how the courts have looked at the reasonableness test.

Mitchell v Finney Lock Seeds (1983) 2 A.C. 803

Here the buyers purchased 30lb of Dutch cabbage seed for £201.60. There was an exemption clause limiting the sellers' liability to the cost of replacement seeds in the event of loss. The seeds turned out to be of the incorrect variety and the buyers lost thousands of pounds in profits. Indeed, by the time the claim reached the House of Lords the claim stood at approximately £100,000!

Remember, the guidelines in Schedule 2 are non-exhaustive. Looking purely from the point of view was the clause reasonable, the courts decided not on the basis that:

(a) it was the seller's fault;
(b) they had in previous cases paid out more than replacement value; and
(c) they could have insured against loss.

The buyers therefore won their claim.

Many cases involving reasonableness have arisen out of the developing of photographs. In *Woodman v Photo Trade Processing* (1981) the defendants accepted films for developing and printing on the basis that the value of such material did not exceed the cost of the material itself and that the developer's liability was limited to the cost of a replacement film. The photographs in question were wedding photos. The claimant received back only 13 negatives. The remaining 23 had been lost. The court decided that the clause seeking to limit liability was unreasonable and awarded £75 damages for distress and disappointment. There does not appear to have been a problem on incorporation but the court clearly thought that most consumers would not take much notice of the clause and that the retailers should not be allowed to rely on it. However, the question was posed, what if the developer provided an alternative, *i.e.* offered merely a replacement film for normal developing rates, but if the consumer paid more he would obtain a higher level of cover. This is sometimes known as the "two-tier" option.

This question was answered in two cases, both reported in *Which?* The Consumers Association Magazine.

(1) *Warren v Truprint* (September 1986); and
(2) *McQuade v Tesco* (November 1988).

In both cases consumers took photographs of important family occasions. When they took them to the developers there was the usual standard clause as outlined above, plus a clause that if a supplementary charge were paid, a higher level of protection would be given. In neither case was the extra charge paid; in both cases the film was lost and in both cases the argument was, did the second clause demanding the extra charge have the effect of making the replacement film clause reasonable?

In both cases the courts felt that consumers would not, just before handing films over (or sending them through the post), hold back and ask for details of an extra service fee. If the fee was prominently set out or details pointed out then the situation could be different.

In both cases the courts decided the clause was unreasonable and in both cases the claimants received £50 damages for distress and disappointment.

Some other cases involving reasonableness that are worth considering are:

Smith v Eric Bush (1990);
Walker v Boyle (1982);
Phillips Products Ltd v Hyland (1987);
St Albans City and District Council v ICL (1996);
Sheffield v Pickfords (1997);
Overland Shoes v Schenkers (1998);
Expo Fabrics (UK) Ltd v Naughty Clothing Co. (2003).

The case of *Stewart Gill Ltd v Horatio Myer & Co. Ltd* (1992) is also worthy of note. It is a commercial rather than a consumer case, but the decision may be relevant to consumer cases in the future. Here the claimants, who were trying to enforce payment, had a clause in the contract that stated "the Customer shall not be entitled to withhold payment of any amount due to the company under the contract by reason of any payment credit set-off counter-claim allegation of incorrect or defective goods OR FOR ANY OTHER REASON WHATSOEVER". On an interlocutory claim, the court decided that these last few words rendered the whole clause unreasonable, the inference being that if the clause had been drafted differently, and not so widely, then parts of it may have been allowed to stand in another form. Clearly, the longer and more complicated the clause, the more chance the whole lot stands to be struck out, whereas if it is split into Clauses 1, 2 and 3 for example, some clauses may survive the reasonableness test.

Terms in the Supply of Goods and Services Act

So far the Sale of Goods implied terms have been discussed and their equivalents under the Supply of Goods (Implied Terms) Act. How does UCTA deal with the implied terms relating to goods governed by the Supply of Goods and Services Act, *i.e.* exchange goods, hire goods or the materials part of a works and materials contract?

Section 7 of the Unfair Contract Terms Act says in relation to these implied terms that, as in section 6, any attempt to exclude them is void where the buyer deals as a consumer and subject to the reasonableness test where the buyer is a non-consumer.

In other words, section 7 works in exactly the same way as section 6. All a student has to know is that if the Supply of Goods and Services Act is involved then, in relation to the goods part, it is section 7 of the UCTA that must be used and not section 6. Thus, if Fred takes his car into a garage to have it serviced, and defective parts have been used and there is an exclusion clause on the signed invoice excluding liability for work and materials then, in respect of the materials, liability cannot be excluded by section 7 where Fred is dealing as a consumer. This work and materials example will be considered at the end of the next section on negligence.

Negligence-based clauses

The second important area where the Unfair Contract Terms Act operates is in relation to negligence-based clauses.

Negligence is defined in section 1 as the breach of a duty of care arising in contract. This includes the section 13 of the Supply of Goods and Services Act term. It also includes the breach of a duty of care in tort or breach of the common duty of care under the Occupiers Liability Act 1957.

As far as consumer law is concerned, the area that is most likely to arise in examinations is an attempt to exclude liability for a breach of section 13 of the Supply of Goods and Services Act. This is a clear attempt to exclude liability for negligence. Section 2 of the Unfair Contract Terms Act says that any clause or notice is ineffective, *i.e.* void in so far as it attempts to exclude liability for negligence resulting IN DEATH OR PERSONAL INJURY. Thus, in the example given earlier, where Fred has his car serviced, suppose this time the parts were not defective but the installation was incorrect. Fred again has a signed invoice excluding liability for work and materials. On his way home, due to the poor workmanship, the brakes failed and he crashed causing himself personal injury. He can sue for a breach of section 13 of the Supply of Goods and Services Act. Once negligence has been proved (do remember this requirement, for if Fred could not prove defective workmanship, there would be no breach of an implied term) then any exclusion clause would be void as the end result damage is personal injury.

Section 2(2) of the Unfair Contract Terms Act goes on to state that if any other loss or damage results then the clause is only valid provided the reasonableness test as outlined earlier is satisfied.

Therefore, if Fred is dissatisfied with the way in which the work has been performed, but does not have a crash and takes the car to be repaired elsewhere, costing him say £100, he could attempt to recover his £100 and any exclusion clause brought in by the first garage would be subject to the reasonableness test as Fred has only suffered financial loss.

Did the work or the materials cause the damage?

It is most important when answering questions involving work and materials to split the answer up as to whether the damage is caused by the work or the materials or both. Remember, if it is the materials and an exclusion, section 7 of the Unfair Contract Terms Act operates, if it is poor workmanship and there is an exclusion, section 2 of the Unfair Contract Terms Act operates.

Other breaches of contract

The third major area where the Unfair Contract Terms Act operates is in relation to other breaches of contract, *i.e.* any other clause in a contract. This is governed by section 3 of the Unfair Contract Terms Act.

Section 3 applies where one party deals as a consumer or on the other party's written standard terms of business. The section applies to a clause whereby that other party:

(a) tries to exclude or restrict his liability in respect of a breach of contract, *e.g.* liability limited to £100 or as in the photo cases liability limited to the cost of a replacement film; or

(b) claims to be entitled to render a contractual performance substantially different from that which was reasonably expected of him, *e.g.* where the management reserves the right to alter any performance or a tour company to alter a holiday; or

(c) claims to be entitled to render no performance at all, *e.g.* seller not liable for non-delivery.

All these clauses are subject to the reasonableness test. Thus it can now be seen why in the photograph cases outlined earlier, the clauses were subject to the reasonableness test.

These are the three most important areas to be dealt with by the Unfair Contract Terms Act.

Other provisions of the Unfair Contract Terms Act

The Act also contains other provisions relating to exclusion clauses.

(a) By section 4, a person dealing as a consumer cannot be made to indemnify another person against liability for negligence or breach of contract unless the clause satisfies the reasonableness test.

(b) Section 5 deals with manufacturers' guarantees and declares that if goods which are ordinarily supplied for private use or consumption prove defective while in consumer use and cause loss or damage as a result of negligence in manufacture or distribution, then any attempt to exclude liability in a guarantee is void.

(c) If a misrepresentation is involved, then any attempt to exclude liability for misrepresentation is only valid provided the reasonableness test is satisfied. Section 3 of the Misrepresentation Act 1967 as amended by section 8 of the Unfair Contract Terms Act.

Criminal liability for exemption clauses

Up to this point only civil liability has been considered in relation to exclusion clauses. The clauses however may involve the seller in criminal liability and it is always worth considering whether extra marks could be gained by bringing these factors into the question.

The Consumer Transactions (Restrictions on Statements) Order 1976 as amended, makes it a criminal offence to use a void exemption clause in a consumer sale of goods or hire purchase contract. Therefore, a notice such as no refunds on any goods sold would render the seller criminally liable. Of course, under the civil law, if the consumer purchased defective goods, then by using section 6 of the Unfair Contract Terms Act, the clause would be void. Note, the order does not apply to transactions governed by the Supply of Goods and Services Act 1982 so although clauses here can be dealt with under the civil law they would not be illegal under this legislation. Also clauses excluding liability for damage resulting from negligence may be void or unreasonable, but they are not illegal under this order.

In *Hughes v Hall* (1981) R.T.R. 430 a notice that said "sold as seen and inspected" was declared illegal but in *Cavendish Woodhouse v Manley* (1984) 148 J.P. 289 "sold as seen" was held not to contravene the order.

The order also makes it an offence to supply goods to a consumer with written exclusion clauses without pointing out that a consumer's statutory rights are unaffected or even if an exclusion clause is not mentioned, if extra rights are given the person giving those rights must make it clear that other statutory rights are unaffected. This is why manufacturers, when they offer to replace goods free of charge, *e.g.* soup, confectionery, must place a statement nearby saying statutory rights are unaffected as of course the consumer's rights in contract are against the store and not against the manufacturer. Under the Enterprise Act 2002, Part 8, the Office of Fair Trading is given responsibility for enforcing this legislation.

THE EEC INTERVENTION, THE UNFAIR TERMS IN CONSUMER CONTRACTS REGULATIONS 1999

In relation to unfair contract terms, like many other areas of consumer protection there are attempts to standardise liability throughout the European Community. This resulted in the E.C. Directive on Unfair Terms in Consumer Contracts which was enacted into our law by statutory instrument known as the Unfair Terms in Consumer Contracts Regulations 1994 (S.I. 1994/3159). The regulations took effect in July 1995. They have now been revoked and replaced by the Unfair Terms in Consumer Contract Regulations 1999 (S.I. 1999/2083). It is important to note that they are in addition to the Unfair Contract Terms Act. A consumer therefore has two lines of attack.

Points to note

(1) The regulations apply to contracts between a business seller or supplier and a consumer. They are limited to contracts for the supply of goods and services. THE REGULATIONS DO NOT APPLY TO CONTRACTS MADE BETWEEN TWO BUSINESSES.

(2) A consumer is a natural person who is acting for purposes that are outside his trade business or profession.

(3) Natural persons cannot be limited companies *i.e.* the consumer has to be a natural person.

(4) The regulations only apply to CLAUSES THAT HAVE NOT BEEN INDIVIDUALLY NEGOTIATED. THEY ONLY COVER STANDARD FORM CONTRACTS. Regulation 5(2) says that a term shall always be regarded as not being individually negotiated where it has been drafted in advance and the consumer has therefore not been able to influence the substance of the term. Even if a specific term has been individually negotiated, the regulations will apply to the rest of the contract if on an overall assessment, it is a pre-formulated contract.

(5) If clauses are not individually negotiated and are contained in a consumer contract then the regulations can apply to any term, they are not limited to exclusion clauses like the Unfair Contract Terms Act.

(6) Regulation 5(1) says that a term is UNFAIR if it causes a significant imbalance in the rights and obligations appearing under the contract to the detriment of the consumer

CONTRARY TO THE REQUIREMENTS OF GOOD FAITH.
(7) The test is FAIRNESS AND GOOD FAITH.
(8) A list of *possible* unfair terms is included in Schedule 2 of the Regulations.
(9) Any term that is unfair is not binding on the consumer.
(10) The rest of the contract stands minus the term.
(11) Contract terms should be drafted in *plain intelligible* language.
(12) Insurance contracts are excluded from by the Unfair Contract Terms Act but they are covered by the regulations. However, the terms that clearly define or circumscribe the insured risk and the insurer's liability are not to be assessed for fairness since these restrictions are taken into account in calculating the premium paid by the consumer.
(13) Regulation 6(2) says that in so far as it is in plain intelligible language, no assessment shall be made of the fairness of any term which:
   — defines the main subject matter of the contract; or
   — concerns the adequacy of the price or remuneration, as against the goods or services sold or supplied. In other words the consumer cannot allege the contract term relating to the price is unfair. If he has concluded a bad price deal he is stuck with it!
(14) Regulations 10 and 12 require the Director-General of Fair Trading to consider any complaint that a contract term drawn up for general use is unfair. The Director may then have regard to any undertakings given as to the continued use of such a term and may, if he considers it necessary, bring proceedings in the High Court for an injunction, against any person appearing to him to be using or recommending the continued use of such a term in contracts concluded with consumers. The 1999 Regulations enable 10 qualifying bodies and the Consumers Association to apply for injunctions in the same way as the Director-General of Fair Trading. In the only case to date to have reached the House of Lords, *Director-General of Fair Trading v First National Bank plc* (2001) the terms in a simple loan agreement were ruled not to be unfair. Most cases are resolved at a much lower level with a request to alter trading terms. The Office of Fair Trading regularly issues bulletins where they have investigated unfair terms

and have required a change to be made to a company's terms of trading. The complaints have involved, among others, local councils, mobile phone companies, and furniture and food retailers. The Office of Fair Trading has also published a very useful "Briefing Note on Unfair Standard Terms". Note: the intervention of the Director-General does not give a civil remedy to the consumer. Consumers will have to pursue their own remedies under UCTA and the Regulations.

(15) Where any seller or supplier claims that a standard term has been individually negotiated, the burden of proof in this respect shall be on the seller or supplier to prove this.

(16) A consumer has the burden of proving that a term is unfair. The Directive contains no provisions as to this but the DTI is content that the burden should lie on the party seeking to take the particular point. In *Falco Finance Ltd v Michael Gough* (1999) certain mortgage penalty clauses were declared to be unfair and unenforceable against the borrower under the 1994 Regulations.

(17) Schedule 2 of the Regulations gives an indicative but non-exhaustive list of terms that may be regarded as unfair.

(18) Regulation 13 provides a new power for the Director-General and the other qualifying bodies to require traders to produce copies of their standard contracts and to give information about their use in order to make it easier to investigate complaints.

Summary

A summary of the Unfair Contract Terms Act is outlined below:

Clauses made void

(a) Where the buyer deals as a consumer the implied terms under sections 13 and 14 of the Sale of Goods Act, sections 9 and 10 of the Supply of Goods (Implied Terms) Act 1973, sections 3, 4, 8 and 9 of the Supply of Goods and Services Act (sections 6 and 7 of the UCTA).

(b) Manufacturers' guarantees (section 5 of the UCTA).

(c) An attempt to exclude liability for death or personal injury resulting from negligence (section 2 of the UCTA).

Clauses made subject to the reasonableness test

(a) Where the buyer deals as a non-consumer the implied terms under sections 13 and 14 of Sale of Goods Act, sections 9 and 10 of the Supply of Goods (Implied Terms)

Act 1973, sections 3, 4, 8 and 9 of the Supply of Goods and Services Act (sections 6 and 7 of the UCTA).
(b) Indemnity clauses.
(c) An attempt to exclude liability for misrepresentation.
(d) Contractual clauses governed by section 3 of the UCTA.
(e) An attempt to exclude liability for negligence where property damage or financial damage results.

REMEMBER

(a) The Unfair Contract Terms Act applies to exclusion clauses contained in business and consumer contracts. The Regulations apply to any term that has not been individually negotiated in a consumer contract.
(b) There are powers under the regulations for the Director-General of Fair Trading and other named organisations to take steps to have unfair terms removed from consumer contracts. There are no similar powers under the Unfair Contract Terms Act.

7. CONSUMER CREDIT

The issues mentioned so far have not involved any discussion of how most consumers finance their purchases but if they do use some form of credit, then how does this affect the transaction and are they given a higher level of protection?

The Consumer Credit Act 1974 was enacted in an attempt to regulate the whole credit industry. It is not the purpose of this text to give a historical analysis of the problems facing the credit industry and consumers, rather this introductory chapter into credit will attempt to set out clearly and concisely the aid given to consumers by the legislation. It is *impossible* to understand the Consumer Credit Act 1974 and its effect on consumers without an appreciation of how basic credit transactions operate and what the definitions in the 1974 Act actually mean.

THE AIMS OF THE ACT

First, the aims of the 1974 Act are:

(a) To regulate the formation, terms and enforcement of credit and hire agreements. It confers certain rights upon consumers and places certain restraints upon the enforcement of an agreement against a consumer.
(b) It sets up a licensing system whereby those engaged in any form of consumer credit business must be licensed. The licensing system applies to many ancillary businesses.
(c) It has provisions designed to secure truth in lending, showing the true cost of credit and the true annual rate of interest.
(d) It controls door-to-door canvassing for credit and creates a number of criminal offences in order to prevent other undesirable methods of seeking credit business.
(e) The Director-General of Fair Trading has the task of administering the licensing system and the general enforcement of the Act. Other enforcement powers are given to Local Trading Standards Officers.
(f) It is impossible to contract out the provisions of the Act as a result of section 173 of the Consumer Credit Act.

Let us therefore look at regulation first of all. As stated earlier, it is impossible to understand credit without a basic appreciation of how various credit transactions work. Once this is understood, then the definitions will be applied. With this in mind, a number of examples have been selected to work through. The examples chosen are:

(1) a hire purchase agreement;
(2) a conditional sale agreement;
(3) a credit sale agreement;
(4) buying goods or services using a credit card;
(5) using a credit card to obtain cash to buy goods or services;
(6) obtaining a loan to buy goods or services and arriving at the lender via the person who supplied the goods or services;
(7) obtaining a personal loan from a bank or other financial institution; and
(8) using an overdraft facility.

These are the most common types of credit transactions to occur in consumer law examinations.

1. Hire purchase

This is a bailment of goods with an option to purchase. What happens in practice is that the consumer (the debtor) wishes to purchase a car, for example from Black and White's Garage, but cannot afford to buy outright. Black and White do all their financing on hire purchase terms via Grasping Finance Ltd. The debtor normally conducts all his negotiations via the garage, selects his car and fills in an offer form with all his financial details. The form is then passed onto the finance company that will check on the debtor's creditworthiness and provided they are satisfied will "accept" the deal. The garage then sells the car to the finance company and it is the finance company that bail the goods out to the debtor with an option to purchase. The debtor therefore is actually contracting with the finance company **NOT** the garage for the purchase of the vehicle so that if the car proves to be defective the debtor's rights under the Supply of Goods (Implied Terms) Act 1973 are exercisable against the finance company. Diagram 1 serves to illustrate this and is known as the HIRE PURCHASE TRIANGLE.

Diagram 1: A hire purchase agreement

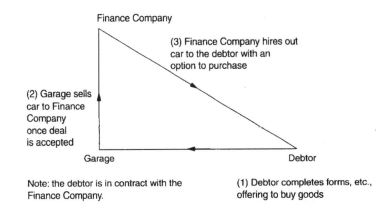

Finance Company

(3) Finance Company hires out car to the debtor with an option to purchase

(2) Garage sells car to Finance Company once deal is accepted

Garage

Debtor

Note: the debtor is in contract with the Finance Company.

(1) Debtor completes forms, etc., offering to buy goods

2. Conditional sale agreement

This is a sale of goods subject to a condition and the condition is that the property will not pass until the goods have been paid for. As in hire purchase, the finance company has legal title to the goods until the last instalment is paid.

A conditional sale agreement works in exactly the same way as a hire purchase agreement, exactly the same steps take place in the transaction and the debtor is once again contracting with the finance company. The only difference to note is that the transaction is governed by the Sale of Goods Act 1979 and NOT the Supply of Goods (Implied Terms) Act 1973.

Diagram 2: A conditional sale agreement

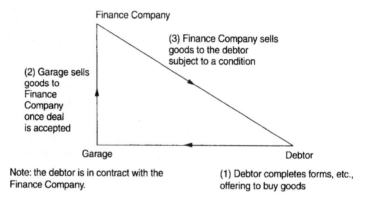

Note: the debtor is in contract with the Finance Company.

(1) Debtor completes forms, etc., offering to buy goods

3. Credit sale agreement

This situation usually occurs when a store is financing its own goods to increase sales. If it is a credit sale agreement then the property passes to the debtor immediately so that, unlike a conditional sale or hire purchase agreement, the finance company has no rights over the goods. Rather than a triangle, as the store is doing its own financing, the credit sale diagram can be done in a straight line.

Diagram 3: Credit sale agreement

[1] Debtor agrees to buy goods ⟶ [2] Store supplies goods and the credit

Store = FINANCIER AND SUPPLIER

The transaction, if it is for goods, is governed by the Sale of Goods Act. It could well be that the consumer is buying services, *e.g.* building work, which he is going to pay for over a number of months. This time, the builder is financing the deal and the transaction is governed by the Supply of Goods and Services Act 1982.

4. Buying goods or services using a credit card

When using a credit card to buy goods or services, the consumer is entering into a contract with the store or the supplier of the work to supply the goods or services. He signs a voucher for the amount of the goods or services. He will have entered into an agreement with a credit card company, *e.g.* Visa, and will have been issued with a card and be subject to an agreed credit limit. He agrees to repay the credit card company whenever he uses the card to purchase goods or services. The store/supplier transmits his credit voucher to the company who will pay out the value less any agreed commission rates.

Diagram 4: Using a credit card to buy goods or services

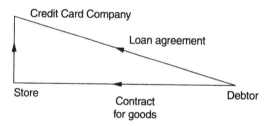

The steps taken are:

(a) contract between the store and the debtor governed by the Sale of Goods Act 1979 (or, if for services by the Supply of Goods and Services Act 1982);

(b) store sends off voucher to credit card company for reimbursement less commission charges. (May be done via other electronic means but important point is that the retailer is reimbursed); and

(c) debtor owes the credit card company the amount for goods or services.

5. Using a credit card to obtain cash

When the credit card is used to withdraw cash, the debtor agrees according to his contract with the credit card company to repay the cash, plus usually a handling charge for the facility. (Handling charges and terms vary between the different card providers.) When the money is used to purchase goods or

services, separate contracts come into existence with the various
suppliers:

(a) debtor uses card to withdraw cash. He owes the money to
    the credit card company;
(b) debtor enters into entirely separate contracts for the
    purchase of goods or services.

6. Obtaining a loan where the loan company is linked to the supplier of the goods or services

When this situation occurs the debtor agrees to purchase goods
or services from, *e.g.* a garage. The garage has an arrangement
with the finance company whereby the finance company agrees
to loan all the garage's clients money to purchase cars. This is
known as a loan-linked agreement. Note the difference between
this kind of arrangement as compared to a hire purchase or
conditional sale agreement. The company loan the debtor the
money (first contract) and the debtor purchases the goods from
the garage (second contract). The loan company usually settles
the amount outstanding direct with the garage. The sale contract
between the debtor and the garage is governed by the Sale of
Goods Act 1979.

Diagram 5: A loan-linked agreement

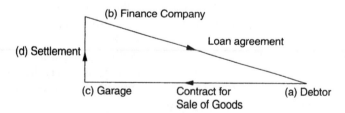

(a) Debtor agrees to buy goods;
(b) contract between loan company and debtor;
(c) sale contract between debtor and garage; and
(d) settlement between garage and finance company.

7. Obtaining a personal loan

Here there is no link between the garage and the finance
company. The debtor agrees to purchase the car and the first

contract is governed by the Sale of Goods Act 1979. Let us say for instance that he obtained a loan from The Good Bank Ltd to finance the transaction. This second contract is a loan and the money is generally credited to the debtor's account.

Diagram 6: A personal loan

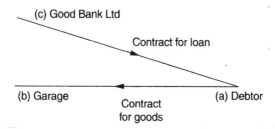

(a) Debtor agrees to purchase goods;
(b) the deal between the debtor and the garage is a contract governed by Sale of Goods Act; and
(c) loan agreement by bank and debtor is a second contract.

8. Overdraft facilities

Here, the debtor has entered into a contract whereby a bank will loan him money up to an agreed limit subject to repayment terms. However, the debtor chooses to spend his money, there is no connection between the bank and the suppliers of the goods or services.

DEFINITIONS

The eight examples outlined above are the most common types of credit transactions that will be encountered in examinations and practice.

The next stage of understanding and appreciating how credit works is to master the definitions under the Consumer Credit Act. The definitions are contained in sections 8 to 20 of the Act and they are vital to answering consumer credit questions. Most of the controls under the Act apply only to a "regulated" agreement.

What is a regulated agreement?

To discover whether an agreement is "regulated" it must come within the definition of a consumer credit agreement contained in section 8 of the Act. The agreement, provided it satisfies section 8, is a regulated one provided it is not exempt under section 16. In other words, the Act does not say what a regulated (a covered agreement under the Act) agreement is, it merely states which agreements are not covered under the Act. If an agreement satisfies section 8 and is not exempt, it is regulated. It is impossible to understand what constitutes an exempt agreement until the definitions are understood therefore, via a circular route, we are able to reach the definition of a regulated agreement.

First, the definition under section 8 will be considered, then the remaining definitions will be looked at in the context of the eight examples given earlier so that the student will become used to categorising agreements immediately and understand the importance of the definitions.

Monetary limits

The starting point for all agreements is to consider the effect of section 8 of the Consumer Credit Act, which defines an agreement. It says it is an agreement by which the creditor provides the individual (and the word individual includes a partnership *but not* a company) with credit not exceeding £25,000. (The original limit of £5,000 set out in the Act now stands by virtue of regulations at £25,000. The Consumer Credit (Increase of Monetary Limits) (Amendment) Order 1998 (S.I. 1998/996).) The monetary limit, currently under review, is therefore the first significant factor to be considered when deciding whether or not an agreement is covered by the Act.

At present, the Act covers agreements where the credit extended is less than £25,000. Many creditors nowadays choose to lend more than £25,000 so that they are not concerned with the Consumer Credit Act and often advertisements will appear stating that the lender will only lend in excess of £25,001.

Fixed sum and running account credit

Often agreements will have a total repayment well in excess of £25,000 when deposits and interest charges are taken into account *but* the significant figure for determining whether or not it is covered by the Act brings in the first definition to be considered, *i.e.* fixed sum credit. Therefore:

(a) If it is fixed sum credit the *significant* figure for determining whether the agreement is within the monetary limits is to consider the amount of money being lent NOT the end result figure on the agreement. FIXED SUM CREDIT is where the amount being lent can be determined at the outset by both the debtor and the creditor so that in the examples given earlier: hire purchase; conditional sales; credit sales; loan-linked and independent loan agreements, these are all examples of fixed-sum credit as the debtor signs an agreement to repay a fixed amount of money. Therefore, the significant figure is the amount of money being lent so that if Jack agrees to buy a car on hire purchase terms for a total price of £30,000 and the figure includes interest charges of £4,000 and a deposit of £3,000 the actual amount of money being lent is £23,000. The agreement is therefore within the Act. Do NOT therefore be misled into starting a question with the words "as the total price exceeds £25,000 the agreement is not covered", remember the *significant* figure is the amount being lent.

(b) Credit is either fixed sum or running account. Fixed sum has been covered above. If the credit is running account, this means that the debtor is given a pre-set credit limit by the creditor and is allowed to "run up" to that amount. Thus, in the examples given earlier, credit cards used to pay for goods and services, or to withdraw cash and overdraft facilities, are all examples of running account credit. Here the significant figure for determining whether it is within the Act is the credit limit. If it is below £25,000, the agreement is covered by the Act. Therefore, most credit cards are covered under this provision.

Running account and fixed-sum credit are defined under the Act in section 10. Because it was felt that some creditors might set artificially high credit limits to avoid the Act, section 10(3) sets out that running account credit will still qualify as a regulated consumer credit agreement if:

(a) the debtor cannot withdraw more than £25,000 at any one time;

(b) the debt exceeds a certain amount and the rate of interest becomes very high; and

(c) at the time of making the agreement it is unlikely that the debit balance will ever exceed £25,000.

Thus, it can be seen that even if the credit limit is higher than £25,000, the agreement may still be covered by the Act. Credit cards should always be studied to see whether or not they are covered by the full protection of the Act. A number of Gold Cards issued by the leading banks may not be covered under the Act because of the amount limits set out in this section.

Restricted-use and unrestricted-use credit

The next definition to be considered is that the agreement must either be restricted-use credit or unrestricted-use credit: section 11 of the CCA. If the debtor's use to which he can put the credit is in some way restricted by the creditor, then the credit is restricted use. As a rough guide, if the debtor is able to place his hands on the money it is unrestricted-use credit.

To take some examples: if it is a hire purchase, conditional sale or credit sale, the creditor will only lend the debtor the money provided that certain goods or services are purchased using it. The debtor ends up with the goods, but never has any money in his hand therefore credit sales, conditional sales and hire purchase are all restricted-use credit. When a credit card is used to buy goods or services the debtor's use to which he can put the card is restricted to those outlets that will take the card. He is therefore obtaining restricted-use credit (albeit he can use the card in thousands of outlets) and again never has any money in his hand.

In the case of a loan-linked agreement (Example 6 above) the loan company will usually settle direct with the garage. Thus, again it is restricted-use credit and the debtor does not receive the money. Where a credit card is used to withdraw cash to pay for goods or services, the credit is unrestricted, the debtor has money in his hand and is free to spend it wherever he chooses.

In the case of a personal loan agreement, the bank credits the debtor with the agreed amount and the debtor writes out a cheque to the garage for instance, in Example 7. The credit here is unrestricted use, as once the debtor has the money in his account, he is free to do with it whatever he wishes. This is so even if he is in breach of contract with the bank, section 11(3), because he has obtained the loan, for example, for a car and has spent it on a holiday. (Of course the bank would only ever express an interest where the debtor failed to make his repayments.)

If, in the case of Example 6, the loan company did credit the account of the debtor and the debtor were to settle matters with the finance company, again the credit would be unrestricted use. Overdraft facilities are of course always unrestricted use.

Debtor-creditor and debtor-creditor-supplier agreements

The next definition (and perhaps the most important one to be considered) is whether the agreement is a debtor-creditor-supplier agreement (referred to as a DCS agreement) or a debtor-creditor agreement (referred to as a DC agreement). Basically, the debtor achieves a much higher level of protection if his credit agreement can be classed as a debtor-creditor-supplier agreement.

It is *absolutely vital* to understand the Consumer Credit Act terminology. The word SUPPLIER means the person with whom the debtor has *legally* contracted to obtain the goods or services from, and NOT the person who actually hands them over. Therefore, in our hire purchase, conditional sale and credit sale examples, the legal supplier is the finance company and NOT the middle man, garage or store. This point cannot be overemphasised.

For an agreement to be a debtor-creditor-supplier one under section 12, there has to be some kind of *business connection* between the supplier and the creditor. This arises in three ways under the Act and is again best illustrated by examples.

(a) Where the supplier and creditor are the same person (section 12(a) of the CCA)

In a hire purchase, conditional sale or credit sale agreement (Examples 1 to 3) the legal supplier of the goods, as stated above, is the finance company. They are also the creditor. What stronger business connection could there be than that the creditor and supplier is the same person? Conditional sale, credit sale and hire purchase are always debtor-creditor-supplier agreements and, as the creditor and the supplier are the same, they are known as two-party debtor-creditor-supplier agreements. Building up on the definitions learnt, hire purchase, credit sale and conditional sales are all examples of two-party debtor-creditor-supplier agreements for restricted-use fixed-sum credit.

(b) Where the supplier and the creditor operate under a restricted-use credit agreement made under pre-existing arrangements

These are loan-linked agreements and credit cards used to purchase goods or services. In both cases the only way the debtor obtained credit to purchase the goods was because of some business arrangement in force between the supplier and the finance company. The only way a consumer can use his credit card in a store is because the store has an arrangement, *e.g.* with Mastercard or Visa. In these two cases (Examples 4 and 6) the creditor and the supplier are different persons so, although the agreement in each case is a debtor-creditor-supplier one, this time it is a three-party DCS agreement. Thus, loan-linked agreements and credit cards can be fully categorised as three-party debtor-creditor-supplier agreements for restricted-use credit. In the case of loan-linked agreements, the credit is fixed sum whereas in the case of credit cards, the credit is running account.

(c) Where unrestricted-use credit is involved and where the creditor under pre-existing arrangements with the supplier credits the debtor, anticipating that the debtor will forward the cash onto the supplier

This is an example of the loan-linked agreement where the creditor credits the debtor and the debtor settles the account with the supplier. If this happens, again because the debtor only "came by" the money because of the link between the creditor and the supplier and used it in the proper manner, he has created a debtor-creditor-supplier agreement. This one can be categorised as a three-party DCS for unrestricted-use fixed-sum credit. It is comparatively rare compared to (a) and (b) above as normally the finance company settles direct with the supplier.

(d) All other agreements are debtor-creditor agreements as there is no link between the supplier and the creditor (section 13 of the CCA)

Thus where credit cards are used to withdraw cash or personal loans, or overdraft facilities are involved, these are all examples of debtor-creditor agreements.

Therefore, all credit agreements need to be categorised into:

(a) price limits;
(b) fixed-sum or running account credit;
(c) restricted-use or unrestricted-use credit;
(d) debtor-creditor or debtor-creditor-supplier agreements; or
(e) two- or three-party debtor-creditor-supplier agreements.

ALWAYS categorise agreements to pick up the maximum amount of marks.

EXEMPT AGREEMENTS

Now that the definitions have been learnt and understood via the circular route, section 16 has been reached, *i.e.* the definition of an exempt agreement. The following are the most important categories of an exempt agreement.

(a) The first four exemptions relate to land mortgages. As a general rule most first land mortgages are outside the ambit of the Act and this text. A number of second mortgages not used to finance the purchase of land will come within the ambit of the Act but again, as they do not usually form the basis of examination questions, they will not be discussed here.

(b) Debtor-creditor-supplier agreements (but not hire purchase or conditional sale agreements) for fixed-sum credit, where the number of payments to be made by the debtor does not exceed four (excluding any deposit) and the credit must be repaid within 12 months of the making of the agreement. In practice, therefore, the only agreements to be exempt are credit sales and loan-linked agreements. It is the intention of this exemption to relieve creditors of much form filling, etc.

(c) Debtor-creditor-supplier agreements for running account credit where the debtor has to repay the balance in a single payment. This affects cards like American Express and Diners Club and some bank Gold Cards where debtors have to repay the whole outstanding balance and cannot, as in the case of Visa or Mastercard, repay part and incur interest on the balance. The fact that these are exempt agreements is of vital importance if, for instance, the goods purchased with the cards are defective because section 75 of the Consumer Credit Act does not apply if the agreement is not regulated. Students should always check in any examination question what kind of card is involved and, if it is unclear, the answer should include a statement saying, "Assuming the card is of the Mastercard/Visa variety, then the agreement is a consumer credit agreement for restricted-use running account credit and is regulated as it is not exempt".

(d) Previously, any debtor-creditor agreement where the cost of credit was very low could be exempt under the Act. This has now been altered by regulations introduced in August 1999 (the Consumer Credit (Exempt Agreements) (Amendment) Order 1999). Now this low-cost credit exemption is only applicable to loans that are not available to the public generally, *e.g.* employer employee loans. The satisfying requirements for this low-cost exemption are set out in detail in the new regulations.

Very competitive pricing is still taking place for instance in the car industry and most manufacturers are advertising new cars at very highly subsidised rates of interest and more often than not at 0 per cent APR. These agreements are debtor-creditor-supplier agreements and have never come within the exempt categories.

Thus, once the exempted agreements are learnt, every other agreement where credit of less than £25,000 is lent is a regulated agreement.

LINKED TRANSACTIONS

The final definition to be considered is that of a linked transaction. Linked transactions are only important in relation to the debtor withdrawing from an agreement or cancelling an agreement. Also, creditors cannot insert terms into linked transactions when they could not have placed them in the main transaction *Citibank International v Schleider* (1999).

Linked transactions are defined by section 19 of the Consumer Credit Act and include transactions entered into in compliance with the principal agreement, *e.g.* the debtor has to take out life insurance or car insurance if he wants the loan or, if it is a three-party debtor-creditor-supplier agreement, then the supply agreement is a linked transaction in relation to the main agreement. This is set out in the diagram below.

Diagram 7: A loan-linked transaction

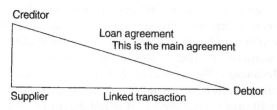

The purpose behind this is that if the debtor can escape from the main agreement then he wants to rid himself of any transactions linked to it.

In the following chapters, now that these definitions have been mastered, the most common kinds of questions both in examinations and practice will be considered.

8. HOW TO "ESCAPE" FROM A CONSUMER CREDIT AGREEMENT

Once the basic definitions of consumer credit have been learnt, questions will arise in one of three ways. Students will be examined on the following issues.

(a) How can a debtor escape as cheaply as possible from a credit agreement?

(b) The goods purchased on credit terms turn out to be defective.

(c) The debtor cannot afford to pay.

[There may be an overlap between (a) and (c).]

Licensing system

The Consumer Credit Act 1974 establishes a licensing system in an attempt to regulate the credit industry. This involves a system of issuing group licences for certain professions (*e.g.* the Law Society has a group licence covering firms for consumer debt advice) and standard individual licences. The Office of Fair Trading has recently announced a review of the group licensing regime. At the time of printing, the fees for a licence are £275 for a company and £110 for an individual or sole trader. The licences last for a period of five years.

Currently, the Office of Fair Trading can refuse an application for a licence or suspend a licence when it considers it fit to do so. New regulations relating to appeals were introduced by the Consumer Credit Licensing (Appeals) Regulations 1998. More recently in May 2003, the government announced plans to modernise consumer credit licensing and to introduce a wider range of sanctions against rogue credit businesses, including fines, undertakings and licensing conditions. Further reforms were announced in December 2003.

Who requires a licence?

Licences are required by:

(a) anyone who lends money not in excess of £25,000 to individuals;

(b) anyone who passes an individual on to a source of finance (a credit broker). This is the middle-man in many of the examples referred to earlier, *i.e.* the store or the garage;

(c) anyone who operates a credit-reference agency (these will be used to check on a person's creditworthiness); and

(d) anyone who gives consumer debt advice.

Sanctions for not having a licence

The sanctions for operating without a licence are both civil and criminal but it is the civil aspect that will be concentrated upon here. If a lender operates without a licence when one is required, then if he wishes to enforce the agreement he will be unable to do so without a validating order from the Office of Fair Trading. (Section 40 of the Consumer Credit Act.) In addition, if the credit broker is unlicensed but the creditor was licensed, once again the agreement is unenforceable without a validating order. (Section 149 of the Consumer Credit Act.) Consumer law students should therefore note how many stores and garages have signs indicating "licensed credit broker".

Therefore, whenever a debtor wishes to escape from an agreement, it is always worth checking on the register kept in London whether or not the creditor or credit broker has a valid licence. If they do not have one, the agreement is unenforceable.

THE FORMAL REQUIREMENTS OF CREDIT AGREEMENTS

It has been seen above that the aim of licensing is to control the credit industry as a whole. Our attention is now turned towards the control of individual agreements. The Consumer Credit Act, mainly in the form of regulations made under sections 60 and 65 of the Act sets out the form credit agreements should take, the size and colour of the printing, etc., and how many copies are required.

The objective of the legislation is to make sure that the debtor is fully aware of all his rights and obligations in as plain English as possible, and if further information is needed, whom he ought to contact, etc.

Sanctions for failure to observe the regulations

If the creditor fails to comply with the formalities, the agreement is said to be "improperly executed". By section 65 of the Consumer Credit Act, the agreement cannot be enforced against the debtor without a court order.

[**Note:** the difference between licensing defects that require a validating order from the Office of Fair Trading, and formality defects that require court orders. Sometimes the defect is regarded as being so bad that the courts have no power to make an order (see, *e.g.* cancellable agreements). This would be a case of the debtor having his cake and being able to eat it! See *Dimond v Lovell* (2000) where the House of Lords ruled that a car-hire agreement was subject to the Consumer Credit Act 1974 and, because it failed to comply with the formalities, it was unenforceable. However, in *National Westminster Bank v Story* (1999), the defendants tried to argue that their loans were irrecoverable for want of compliance with the formalities. In this case the Court of Appeal said that three separate agreements were held to have been agreed as one transaction. This took the credit limit over the amount covered by the Consumer Credit Act. Because the credit limit was exceeded, the agreements were not regulated by the Consumer Credit Act and therefore no statutory formalities were required. The defendants had to repay the loans.]

Formalities

Sections 60 and 61 enable regulations to be made to ensure the debtor is made aware of his obligations and rights. The many details are found in the Consumer Credit (Agreements) Regulations 1983 as amended. Agreements (depending on their type) should make it clear *inter alia*:

(a) the amount and timing of repayments;
(b) the Annual percentage Rate (APR) (total charge for credit); and
(c) the protection and remedies available to the debtor under the Act.

The copy provisions

This must be learnt and again the student is reminded of the necessity of knowing contract law. The Act sets out when and how many copies of an agreement a debtor should receive. The provisions are contained in sections 62 and 63.

Let us take a typical hire purchase example to illustrate the effect of the formalities.

Martin wishes to purchase a new Trissan car from Damalls under a hire purchase agreement. He will complete the forms at the garage with details of the car, his income and the anticipated monthly repayments. At this stage, Martin is merely making an offer to purchase the car. No formal contract is concluded until the information is passed onto the finance company and they have accepted him after checking out his creditworthiness. In Consumer Credit Act terminology, Martin's offer means that he has an "unexecuted" agreement of a prospective regulated agreement. Martin must, in this situation, be given a copy of what he has signed (section 62(1)).

When the deal is accepted by the finance company, a copy of the executed agreement must be delivered or sent within seven days (section 63(2)).

Therefore, if the agreement is *unexecuted at the outset* Martin should end up with *two* copies.

Suppose, however, it is sale time and instant credit is on offer. In a number of situations the garage/store will be authorised by either their own financier, or an outside creditor to conclude deals on the spot provided that they do not exceed a certain amount and that certain basic credit checks are made there and then. In that case, the agreement is executed, offer and acceptance has occurred, the debtor is bound and is entitled to just one copy of the agreement (section 63 (1) and (2)).

Summary

Where the agreement is unexecuted the debtor receives *two* copies, where the agreement is executed only *one* copy *is* required to comply with the formalities.

In the case of a cancellable agreement (this is discussed below) changes are made to the copy provisions:

(a) every copy must contain a notice in the prescribed form, telling the debtor of the right of cancellation, how to exercise it, and to whom it should be sent;

(b) in cases where a second copy is required (*i.e.* where the agreement is unexecuted at the outset) the second copy must be sent by post (section 63(3)). (So that no pressure is put on the debtor);

(c) in cases where a second copy is not required (*i.e.* where the agreement is executed) then if the agreement is cancellable, a notice detailing the cancellation rights must be sent through the post to the debtor within seven days.

In the case of a cancellable agreement, if the requirements of (a), (b) and (c) above are not complied with, the "unenforceability" sanction is particularly severe, *i.e.* the creditor will be unable to enforce the agreement. (Section 127(4).) *Moorgate Services v Kabir* (1995).

Withdrawal

One of the cheapest ways of escaping from an agreement is to argue that there is in fact no agreement in existence between the seller and buyer, *i.e.* that offer and acceptance have not occurred.

Looking back at the formalities, whenever a debtor enters into a credit agreement, remember that if the agreement is unexecuted at the time, the debtor is entitled to a copy of the offer he has made. Suppose Bill agreed yesterday to purchase a TV and video on hire purchase terms from Bewis's. Grasping Finance Ltd service all their agreements. The agreement is unexecuted. Today Bill consults you, saying he has made a mistake and wants to escape from the agreement. Provided that his "offer" has not been accepted by the finance company, he can withdraw from the agreement using basic contractual rules.

Obviously, he has to notify the creditor (or the credit broker, Bewis's) as notice of revocation must be given before acceptance. This notice can be given orally. This is the *effect* of section 57 of the Act.

[**Note:** that as revocation must be communicated to the offeree before acceptance it would be bad advice to rely on the post alone as acceptance could occur before the letter is received.]

Cancellation

Assuming that the licensing requirements have been met and all the formalities properly complied with so that the agreement has been properly executed, the final "cheap" way of escaping from an agreement is to see whether or not it is a cancellable one.

Normally, where offer and acceptance have occurred, the agreement is concluded and is binding on the parties. However, we are now about to discover a situation where, although all the elements of contract law appear to have been satisfied, the consumer debtor is able to escape from the agreement by virtue of the provisions of section 67 of the Consumer Credit Act.

Section 67 was originally drafted to "get at" doorstep sales and offer the pressurised consumer an escape route once they had been persuaded to sign an agreement. However, it has been drafted in wide terms and covers situations other than doorstep sales.

What is a cancellable agreement?

By section 67, where *oral representations* have taken place in antecedent negotiations in *the debtor's presence* AND the agreement has been signed away from the trade premises of the creditor, the negotiator (*i.e.* the supplier or credit broker) or a party to a linked transaction, then the agreement is cancellable.

Antecedent negotiations

Antecedent negotiations, as defined by section 56 of the Consumer Credit Act, include anything said about the goods or credit by the creditor or the credit broker or the supplier. For the cancellable agreement provisions, these must have taken place IN THE DEBTOR'S PRESENCE. Telephone negotiations are therefore not covered as it is easy for the debtor merely to put the telephone down.

It is easy to fulfil the requirements of the first part of this section as, in most consumer transactions, the buyer will, for example, in buying a car, visit the car showroom and ask various things about the car. There have therefore been antecedent oral representations. Note: the wording is antecedent representations and not misrepresentations.

The second requirement is that of signing away from the creditor's business premises, etc. Therefore, once the buyer is allowed to take the agreement home for signature, the agreement is cancellable even though no pressure has been placed on the buyer to sign. This is so even if the buyer is a sole trader and signs on his business premises.

Therefore, if Joanna wishes to purchase a television for £600, including interest charges from Electric Ltd on a credit sale agreement, discusses the deal with the salesman and asks if she can take the forms home to check everything and then signs them at home, the agreement is cancellable. (From the trader's point of view, do not allow consumers to take forms away from the premises.) If Joe, a sole trader, wishes to buy a car but says he is too busy to sign the agreement and could a salesman "drop" it off at his office, the agreement would again be cancellable.

When does the cancellation or cooling-off period start and how long does it last?

Remember, if the agreement was unexecuted, then the debtor should receive, through the post, within seven days of acceptance, a second copy. Both the first and second copy should contain a notice of cancellation rights. If the agreement was executed at the outset then, although in normal circumstances no second copy is required, a separate notice of cancellation rights must be sent through the post to the debtor within seven days.

It is the receipt of either the second copy or notice of cancellation rights which triggers the cooling-off period. This period is *five* days following the day the second copy or notice was received, so that if Joe receives his notice on Saturday he has until Thursday evening to cancel. Therefore, by the time Joe is able to cancel he may well, from a practical point of view, have had the goods for almost a fortnight.

The aim of cancellation is to restore the parties to the position they would have been in had the agreement never been concluded. Thus, goods are returned and payments handed back. It should be pointed out from the retailer's point of view that:

(a) they should not allow the debtor to take the forms away and make agreements cancellable if it is at all possible not to do so; and

(b) they certainly should not allow the debtor to take the goods away until the cooling-off period has expired.

Therefore suppliers will suffer as the goods they recover can no longer be classed as new.

How to exercise cancellation rights

Notice must be exercised in writing, section 69 (see the difference between this and notice of withdrawal). It is valid from the time of posting (and even if it gets lost) and is normally served on the creditor or the credit broker or supplier or someone named in the notice.

The effects of cancellation

In the case of a debtor-creditor-supplier agreement, all monies paid by the debtor must be returned to him. He must make the goods available for collection although he has no positive duty to redeliver. He also has a 21-day duty of care in respect of the goods so any damage caused through negligence must be paid for, section 72(8).

If the agreement is a three-party debtor-creditor-supplier agreement for restricted-use credit, then the creditor and the supplier are jointly and severally liable to repay any monies, section 70(3).

If there is a part exchange involved, particularly where cars are concerned, then under section 73 once the debtor has cancelled the agreement, the negotiator (the credit broker or the supplier) must hand back the part exchange car or its equivalent monetary value within 10 days. Again, if it is a three-party debtor-creditor-supplier agreement, both the creditor and the supplier are jointly and severally liable. In all cases outlined above, the debtor has a lien over the goods until he receives all his money back.

Examples

Some examples will best illustrate these statutory provisions:

(a) Vera chooses a car from Doug's Garage, to be financed by a loan-linked agreement with Ridley Finance Ltd. Doug takes Vera's Bastra car in part exchange for £1,000 and the balance is financed via the loan agreement. Vera takes delivery of her new car under a cancellable agreement, has it for three days and then cancels. Vera must make the car available for collection. Doug or Ridley Finance Ltd must either return Vera's car or its monetary value within 10 days as this is a three-party debtor-creditor-supplier agreement. Any monies paid over by Ridley Finance Ltd must be returned.

(b) Gail buys a TV set from Ivystores, financed by a loan of £270 from Don Ltd, a connected lender. Gail pays a deposit of £30 and takes delivery after paying her first instalment of £20 to Don Ltd. She then cancels. This is a three-party debtor-creditor-supplier agreement. Gail must make the set available for collection. She is entitled to receive the £30 deposit back from either Don Ltd or Ivystores as is the case with the £20 as they are both jointly and severally liable. If Gail had damaged the set in any way she would have been liable for the cost of repair under section 72(8).

Cancellation of linked transactions

Any linked transactions are normally automatically cancelled but in two important instances, by virtue of Consumer Credit (Linked Transactions) (Exemptions) Regulations 1983 the debtor will have to take positive steps to cancel. These are in respect of contracts of insurance and guarantee. So if any insurance was involved, the debtor will have to cancel it.

Cancellation of debtor-creditor agreements

In the case of a mere debtor-creditor agreement, *i.e.* a loan that is cancellable, the debtor may cancel as before. All the transactions he has spent his loan monies on will stand as they are not linked transactions and he is liable to repay the monies (he cannot therefore have his cake and eat it!) but if he repays the loan within one month or by the first repayment date, then no interest charges will be incurred. (Section 71 of the Consumer Credit Act.)

It can be seen that section 71 is only of any value where the debtor has found another cheaper source of finance, or won the pools or the lottery!

In the section above on credit agreements we have seen that there is an escape route for someone buying under a cancellable credit agreement.

WHAT IF CASH IS EMPLOYED AS THE METHOD OF PAYMENT?

The Consumer Protection (Cancellation of Contracts Concluded Away from Business Premises) Regulations 1987 as amended may assist a consumer. These regulations have been enacted pursuant to a European Directive in an attempt to standardise liability throughout the European Community.

The regulations provide for a seven-day cooling-off period, during which agreements covered by the regulations can be cancelled by the customer without penalty. Traders are required to give their customers written notice of the right of cancellation and the name and address of a person against whom it can be exercised. If this is not done, the agreement will be void and unenforceable against the customer. The amendments to the regulations in 1998 now make it a criminal offence where the seller fails to give written details of the right to cancel.

Contracts covered

Where goods and services cost more than £35 and the contract results from an *unsolicited visit* by the trader to the customer's home or place of work (unsolicited means a visit that does not take place at the *express request* of the customer, *i.e.* a visit that has not clearly been initiated by the customer).

[**Note:** this includes a visit that results from an unsolicited telephone call by a trader, during which an appointment is agreed or a further visit resulting from a first unsolicited visit.]

There are a number of exempted contracts, *e.g.* the construction of buildings but agreements for the repair or improvement of property are covered. The Department of Trade and Industry has published useful information on this legislation in the leaflet "Doorstep Selling".

How does the customer exercise his right of cancellation?

By serving written notice on the trader during the time within the cooling-off period.

Contracting out

Any attempt to contract out of the regulations is void.

INTERNET SHOPPING

Shopping over the internet has now become a well-established practice. Consumers are given extra protection when buying goods or services over the internet by virtue of the Consumer

Protection (Distance Selling) Regulations 2000, in addition to their rights under the Sale of Goods Act.

When purchases are made, the legislation sets out the information all buyers should be given about their order and the company. The buyer is given a right to cancel, "a cooling-off period". The regulations also give protection against credit card fraud and provide for remedies in the case of unsolicited goods.

The cooling-off period

Goods   The law provides for a seven-working-day right to cancel after the day on which the goods are received.

Services   The law provides for a seven-working-day right to cancel after the day on which the buyer agreed to go ahead with the contract.

As usual there are special cases relating to goods and services where there are no cancellation rights. For example, betting services and sealed video recordings or CDs that have been opened. The regulations should be checked for these exemptions.

The regulations also apply to shopping by telephone, mail order, fax or digital television.

---

9. LIABILITY FOR DEFECTIVE GOODS PURCHASED ON CREDIT TERMS

The second most common situation involving a complaint by the debtor is that the goods he has purchased using some form of credit turn out to be defective. Is there any way in which the creditor can become involved in an action for defective goods?

Let us approach the question by using a number of examples.

1. Using an overdraft

Martin purchases a television from Bumbelows for £300. He has an overdraft facility with the bank and withdraws the money to pay for the TV set.

The credit in this case is therefore supplied under a debtor-creditor agreement for unrestricted-use running account credit. There is no connection between the bank and Bumbelows. If the television proves defective then Martin's only remedy lies under the Sale of Goods Act 1979 against Bumbelows for a breach of the condition of satisfactory quality. There is no possible question of involving the creditor.

2. Hire purchase and conditional sale agreements

Martin purchases the television under a hire purchase agreement from Bumbelows. Grasping Finance Ltd finance all their transactions. The salesman told Martin that the set was the most reliable model they had in stock. It broke down four times in the first month and could not be repaired. Martin has paid his first instalment of £40.

This time, due to the hire purchase triangle, Martin's contract is with Grasping Finance Ltd. The hire purchase agreement is a two-party debtor-creditor-supplier agreement for restricted-use fixed-sum credit.

Martin's rights are all exercisable against the finance company for a breach of section 10 of the Supply of Goods (Implied Terms) Act 1973 relating to satisfactory quality and fitness.

Martin is entitled to reject the goods for a breach of section 10. There is no doctrine of acceptance, only affirmation. He can recover his £40 and is released from paying future instalments.

In addition, it could be that the salesman at Bumbelows has made various misrepresentations about the goods (it could however be construed as mere sales talk). Using section 56 of the Consumer Credit Act, this says that where a negotiator (here the store) in antecedent negotiations (words spoken about the goods or credit before the conclusion of the deal) makes representations about the goods then he does so not only in his own capacity but as agent for the creditor. Liability cannot be avoided for this provision so that the creditor is directly liable for everything the salesman/middleman has said. This provision is especially useful in a hire purchase or conditional sale transaction.

Everything that has been said above is equally applicable to a conditional sale agreement, except that if the goods are defective then the statute that applies is the Sale of Goods Act.

3. Credit card transactions where goods or services are purchased

Martin purchased a television set from Scurrys for £300 using his Barcess credit card. His credit limit is £4,000. The card is of the type like Mastercard and Visa. The television set breaks down after two months.

When Martin returned to the store to complain he discovered that they had gone into liquidation. He settled his Barcess account in full at the end of last month. Martin has entered into a three-party debtor-creditor-supplier agreement for restricted-use running account credit. His contract with the store is governed by the Sale of Goods Act 1979 and there would appear to be a breach of the implied conditions as to satisfactory quality and fitness of purpose.

Here, because there is a three-party debtor-creditor-supplier agreement for restricted-use credit, the cash price of the goods is between £100 and £30,000 and the agreement is regulated, section 75 of the Consumer Credit Act applies. This is a vitally important provision.

(a) Section 75 only applies to three-party debtor-creditor-supplier agreements. It does not apply to hire purchase, credit sale or conditional sale agreements.

(b) Section 75 only applies where the agreement is regulated (so your answer would clearly be different where the card was of the American Express or Diners Club variety as these are exempt agreements under the Act) and the cash price of the goods is between £100 and £30,000.

(c) Section 75 says that where the debtor has a claim in either contract or misrepresentation against the supplier, he has a like claim against the creditor.

In this case, therefore, Martin has a claim in contract against the creditor by virtue of a breach of the Sale of Goods Act, the price limits are satisfied. Martin can therefore use section 75 as a sword to recover the £300.

[**Note:**

(a) Martin is free to pursue his action at any time against Barcess. The retailer does not have to have gone into liquidation, the retailer may just be unco-operative.

(b) The creditor is liable to the extent that the supplier would have been liable, not just for the amount of credit extended to the debtor, *e.g.* Martin could have used his credit card to leave a £50 deposit and paid the balance in cash. Barcess would still be liable for £300.

The television set could have exploded causing personal injuries to Martin. Martin could have sued Scurrys for the set and his injuries in contract. He could therefore sue the creditor for these amounts.

In the 1995 report on Connected Lender Liability published by the Office of Fair Trading, it was recommended that in the case of credit card transactions, the card issuer should only be liable to the extent of the amount charged to the card account and not for the extra amounts as stated above. This proposal has not been enacted.

(c) Martin might not have settled his credit card account. Can he use section 75 as a shield to avoid payment? To date there is no English authority on the point, but in the Scottish case of *United Dominions Trust v Taylor* (1980) Mr Taylor purchased a car from a garage with the assistance of a loan from UDT. He had been passed on to UDT by the garage, so there was a connected lender three-party debtor-creditor-supplier situation. Mr. Taylor paid nothing under the agreement, felt his car was a "heap of junk" and when the garage refused to do anything about it, he abandoned the car on the forecourt. UDT sued him for defaulting on the loan. Mr Taylor used section 75 as a defence, claiming the money had been used to purchase defective goods and his claim was upheld by the courts. Although this decision has been attacked academically, from a consumer's point of view it seems a perfectly sensible solution. The case can be put forward as authority that section 75 can be used as a defence. Another recent Scottish case, *Forward Trust v Hornsby* (1996), has confirmed *UDT v Taylor*.

4. Loan-linked agreements

Martin purchased a new car from News Garage Ltd for £8,000 with the assistance of a loan of £6,000 from Grasping Finance Ltd. He had been passed onto the finance company by News Garage. With interest charges of £1,200 the total loan repayable was £7,200. Martin paid a £2,000 deposit to News Garage.

After three weeks the engine "seized up" and News Garage were only prepared to repair the car. Martin did not want this. In this case Martin's contract for the car is governed by the Sale of Goods Act 1979 and he would have all the usual rights for a breach of satisfactory quality as outlined earlier. Martin could have a claim in contract against News Garage for £8,000 and interest charges incurred. Because of the loan, he has entered into a three-party debtor-creditor-supplier agreement for restricted-use fixed-sum credit. The cash price of the goods is between £100 and £30,000 and the agreement is regulated as it is credit of less than £25,000 to an individual and it is not exempt.

Section 75 therefore applies. Where the debtor has an action in contract, as here for £8,000 plus, he has a like claim against the creditor. This is *not* limited to the amount of the money he has borrowed, *i.e.* £6,000, but includes *any* contractual claim he may have against the supplier. Therefore, if Martin is having problems with the garage, he could sue the finance company for the return of his £2,000 and resist a claim from the finance company by using section 75 as a defence. See *UDT v Taylor* (1980).

It can be seen that it is therefore advantageous to use section 75 as a means of having another potential defendant to draw into the action when things go wrong. It is particularly useful to pay deposits using a credit card so that if the supplier company does go into liquidation the monies can be recovered from the credit card company.

5. Loan agreement

If Martin had gone to the bank for a loan to enable him to purchase the car, then again as in Example 1, his only remedy would be against the garage as it is a debtor-creditor agreement. He would remain liable to pay the loan.

6. Conditional sale agreement

A conditional sale agreement has been dealt with in point 2 above.

Thus, it can be seen that buying goods using a form of credit can be very useful to a consumer where defective goods are involved.

10. THE DEBTOR IS IN FINANCIAL DIFFICULTIES

The final set of examination questions arise from the situation where the debtor cannot afford his credit repayments. The creditor should, from a practical point of view, always be notified to see whether any accommodation can be reached before the situation reaches crisis point.

Naturally, the course of action to be taken does depend upon whether the debtor wishes to keep the goods or to rid himself of them. Assuming the debtor wishes to rid himself of the goods, the cheap ways out of the agreement which were discussed earlier should be considered, *e.g.* lack of licence, cancellable agreements, etc., but if nothing can be done under these headings then a solution that inevitably will cost money may be found.

First, the type of credit agreement must be considered

(a) If it is a loan, then the overriding principle is that it has to be repaid. There is no way out for the debtor unless the goods are defective and it is a loan-linked agreement. His only remedy will lie in the fact that he may be given more time to pay and this will be explained later.

(b) If it is a hire purchase or conditional sale agreement, then the finance company has legal title to the goods and one of the options open to a debtor who does not wish to keep the goods is to exercise his rights to terminate under sections 99 to 100 of the Consumer Credit Act 1974.

Termination

Termination is a costly option and should be a last resort as it is expensive and the debtor ends up with nothing. **It is only available where the credit agreement is a hire purchase or conditional sale agreement.** For termination to operate under section 99:

(a) the agreement must be regulated under the Consumer Credit Act;

(b) it is available at any time before the final payment falls due;

(c) all arrears must be paid; and

(d) the debtor is liable to pay the creditor half of the total price.

Some examples will serve to illustrate these points.

Example 1

Gill buys a music system for a total price of £2,804 in November. This is done using a hire purchase agreement with Grasping Finance Ltd being the creditor. The total price figure includes a deposit of £500 and interest charges of £350. The balance is repayable by 24 payments of £96. Gill pays one instalment in December, then loses her job and falls into arrears. She visits you in April, now being three months in arrears. One of Gill's options is to terminate. As the total price is £2,804 the starting half point figure is £1,402. Gill has paid £596, being the deposit plus one instalment. This leaves a balance of £806 to pay *including the arrears*. Gill has to clear the arrears which total £288 but in section 100(3) there is a proviso that states if a case does come before the courts, and the court is satisfied that a sum less than one half would be equal to the loss suffered by the creditor, then it may order a lesser amount. Gill can try to argue that because the finance company is receiving almost new goods back quickly, paying them the arrears of £288 should satisfy them. She must be prepared however to pay the full balance of £806 and hand the goods back. It can therefore be seen that termination is a costly option.

Remember always to check your total price figure, divide by two, all arrears must be cleared and the remaining balance taking the figure to one half must be reached. Negotiations can be tried on this remaining balance where the goods are relatively new, but the debtor must be advised of his potential liability to pay the full half figure.

Example 2

Cecil purchases a car on a conditional sale agreement for a total price of £12,500 including interest charges. He gives a £1,700 deposit, leaving the balance repayable by 36 monthly instalments of £300. After 15 months he loses his job and falls into arrears. He visits you for advice when he is two months in arrears. This time, the total price being £12,500, half equals £6,250. He has paid £1,700 plus £4,500 making a total of £6,200.

He only has to pay £50 to terminate, but owes £600 in arrears. If he clears the arrears of £600, this will end his liability. Remember, all arrears have to be cleared.

Example 3

Jane has a hire purchase agreement on her washing machine for £600 including interest charges of £150. Jane pays a £120 deposit with the balance repayable over two years. After paying for three months she is unable to keep up the repayments. She visits you, being one payment in arrears. The total price is £600, half the total price equals £300. Jane has paid £180 and is therefore liable to pay a further £120 including the arrears. If she wishes to terminate, again she must clear the arrears but can attempt to negotiate on the balance, but must be warned of her liability to pay the full amount.

Example 4

If an installation charge is involved, then the half figure that must be reached is the installation charge in full, plus half the remaining balance. Thus, in the example above, assume the £600 figure included a £30 installation charge and Jane again wishes to terminate. This time the half figure would be £600 minus £30 = £570. Divide the remaining balance by two = £285, and add back the installation charge which brings the total to £315. Therefore, this time if Jane wishes to terminate she will have to find £135 instead of £120.

Where the debtor wishes to retain the goods

All of the above examples have been given on the basis that the debtor wishes to get rid of the goods, but what of the debtor who wishes to hang on to the goods, despite being in financial difficulties?

Again, the advice depends on the type of credit agreement. If the agreement is a loan, either loan-linked or arranged independently, it must be repaid. The goods purchased are the debtor's and, if necessary, he can sell them to repay the loan. If a debtor under any kind of credit agreement gets into difficulties, then he will receive a default notice from the credit company under section 87 of the Act.

This notice must be served before the creditor can enforce his rights under the agreement. The default notice must say what the breach is, what must be done to remedy it, and give the debtor at least seven days to put it right. (Sections 87 and 88 Consumer Credit Act.) For our purposes here, once the debtor has received a default notice he can apply to court under section 129 for what is known as a time order.

Time orders

What this does in effect is give the debtor more time to clear his arrears so that if he wishes to keep the goods he should do this.

Normally, time orders only relate to arrears so if the debtor has a loan he will have a longer time to pay (and obviously more interest charges) but in the case of a hire purchase or conditional sale agreement the time order can relate to future payments (section 130(2) of the Consumer Credit Act) so that in effect the whole agreement has been rewritten.

Special help for debtors in a hire purchase and conditional sale agreement

Remember, if the debtor has a hire purchase or conditional sale agreement he does not own the goods. The finance company is the owner. If the debtor wishes to retain the goods, then one tactic he can try is to make the goods "protected". This means that the creditor will have to obtain a court order before the goods can be seized and inevitably this takes time and will give the debtor more time to try to get out of his financial difficulties.

Protected goods

Under section 90 of the Consumer Credit Act goods are protected:

(a) If the debtor has paid more than one-third of the total price.

[**Note:** the difference between termination that is a half and protected goods that is one-third.]

The same rules apply to calculating one-third and installation charges, *i.e.* Joanna buys a cooker on hire purchase for £390 including a £30 installation charge and interest charges of £50. One-third = (£390 minus £30 divided by three) = £120. The installation charge is then

added back in, so if Joanna wanted to make the goods
protected £150 would be the target figure.

(b) The debtor must be in breach (she would be as she is in
    arrears).
(c) The agreement must not have been terminated.
(d) The property must be in the creditor.

What if protected goods are taken back?

If the creditor does seize the goods back without a court order
when more than one-third has been paid, the agreement termi-
nates and the debtor can recover all her payments—another case
of the debtor having their cake and eating it! (Section 91 of the
Consumer Credit Act.)

Therefore, one piece of advice that can be given to debtors is
to try to make the goods protected.

However, it should also be noted that regardless of how little
has been paid, if a creditor has to enter any premises he must
obtain a court order so in any event, as the cooker is on Joanna's
premises, a court order would have to be obtained. (Section 92
of the Consumer Credit Act.) Protected goods provisions are
therefore of most use in the case of motor vehicles frequently
left parked on the roadside.

One last matter that ought to be taken into consideration is
that section 173(3) of the Act says "where a court order or a
validating order by the Director-General is required, the consent
of the debtor given at the time will be equally effective".
Obviously there could be an issue of "true consent" and earlier
cases on older credit legislation have considered this but clearly
a consumer who wishes to retain his goods should not be
advised to hand them back.

Extortionate credit bargains

Finally, in the context of "I can't afford to pay" the issue of
extortionate credit bargains under sections 137 to 140 must be
considered. This is a concept introduced by the Act in 1978 but
it is currently under review. The government has declared it is
determined to outlaw sharp practices in this area and new
legislation is anticipated in the near future.

The current extortionate credit bargain provisions in the Act
are unusual in that:

(a) they apply even if the credit exceeds £25,000; and
(b) even if the agreement is exempt.

The only criteria is that the debtor must be an individual.

What bargains are extortionate?

Section 138 states that a bargain is extortionate if it requires the debtor to make payments that are grossly exorbitant or otherwise grossly contravene ordinary principles of fair dealing.

A *non-exhaustive* list of relevant factors is then set out. These include *inter alia*:

(a) prevailing interest rates at the time the bargain was made;
(b) factors *affecting the debtor, e.g.* age, health, business capacity; (questions in this area often involve John, an elderly pensioner, signed a credit agreement with an APR of 100 per cent); and
(c) factors *affecting the creditor* such as his relationship with the debtor and the degree of risk undertaken.

The debtor can take proceedings through the county court to have the bargain re-opened. Section 171(7) provides that if the debtor alleges that the bargain is extortionate, the onus is on the creditor to prove that it is not, *e.g. Bank of Baroda v Shah* (1988).

If the court decides the bargain is extortionate, it can re-write the agreement. Every case will depend on its own facts. See, *e.g. Ketley v Scott* (1981), *Davies v Direct Loans* (1986) and *Falco Finance Ltd v Michael Gough* (1999).

The debtor with surplus funds

So far we have considered the debtor who is in financial difficulties. However, to finish this section, what about the debtor who wishes to repay a credit agreement early because he has a surplus of funds? Under section 94 there is a non-excludable right to do this. The debtor will *not* receive a rebate on the *full* amount of interest but will receive some rebate using the appropriate tables. (Section 95 of the Consumer Credit Act.) Sections 94 and 95 are currently under review with legislation expected shortly to ensure consumers are made fully aware of their rights and regulations are to be introduced limiting charges in this area.

Lost credit cards

This is governed by section 84 of the Consumer Credit Act. The debtor should notify the card company immediately by telephone of the loss. This must usually be confirmed in writing. The debtor remains liable for the first £50 if the card is misused prior to notification, so the faster the credit card company is notified, the better. If the debtor gave the card to a third party and the card was misused, the debtor remains liable without limit.

---

11.   CONSUMER HIRE AGREEMENTS

As well as covering credit agreements, the Consumer Credit Act also covers hire agreements (section 15 of the Consumer Credit Act). See *Dimond v Lovell* (2000). It is intended in this chapter to highlight problems relating to hired goods.

In recent times, some organisations have reported a large increase in consumers deciding to hire goods as compared to buying them. Many retailers have reported a large increase in the hiring sector, as more consumers work out it may be cheaper for them to rent a washing machine for, say, £30 a month and have all their repair bills covered and a prompt call-out service.

Defective hired goods

Of course, if the goods are defective or do not match their description, etc., there is no breach of the Sale of Goods Act as there has been no transfer of property. Hire goods are governed by Part I of the Supply of Goods and Services Act 1982 (sections 7 to 9). These sections state that hired goods must match their description, be of satisfactory quality and be fit for their purpose.

Exclusion clauses

Exclusion notices are caught by section 7 of the Unfair Contract Terms Act if there is an attempt to exclude liability for description, fitness for purpose or satisfactory quality.

When does the Consumer Credit Act apply?

Hire agreements are caught by the Act if:

(a) there is a bailment of goods;
(b) by one person (the owner);
(c) to an individual;
(d) which is not hire purchase;
(e) which is capable of lasting for more than three months; and
(f) does not require the hirer to pay more than £25,000.

Therefore, agreements such as those for washing machines, videos, satellite dishes and televisions all come within the ambit of the Act.

Termination of the agreement

This is governed by section 101 of the Consumer Credit Act. This gives a statutory right to the hirer to terminate it after 18 months, even if the hiring was for a fixed term of a longer period. (Obviously, if the hirer can terminate under the actual agreement before 18 months, this will take priority.)

Termination only operates for the future and sums that have accrued due must be paid. The hirer must give a termination notice that is equivalent to the shortest payment interval, or three months, whichever is less. So, if the washing machine was on a two-year rental with payments every two months, the hirer could give notice to terminate at the end of month 16.

There are some exemptions in section 101(7), but these relate mainly to commercial equipment. Also, the above termination rights do not apply to any agreement under which the total of hire payments to be made in any year exceeds £1,500.

Section 101(8) has been added by the Enterprise Act 2002. This allows a consumer hire business to apply to the Office of Fair Trading for a notice that this section on termination will not apply to their consumer hire agreements. Conditions can be specified by the Office of Fair Trading.

12.   THE TRADE DESCRIPTIONS ACT

In previous chapters, the civil law relating to the consumer has been considered. The following chapters on pricing, unsafe goods, food safety and trade descriptions involve criminal liability and cover how the intervention of the criminal law can assist the consumer.

It has already been noted that the way in which goods are described is a great influencing factor on what persuades consumers to buy goods. If the description is wrong, then there can be a breach of section 13 or a possible action in misrepresentation. The incorrect description can also give rise to criminal liability under Trade Descriptions Act 1968.

If a conviction is obtained under the Act, then under the Powers of Criminal Courts (Sentencing) Act 2000, section 131, compensation of up to £5,000 per offence can be obtained for the consumer.

Using the Act could therefore be a cheaper, easier way of obtaining compensation than taking a claim before the civil courts.

BASIC REQUIREMENTS OF THE ACT

The Act operates in two areas:
    (1) in relation to goods; and
    (2) in relation to services.

GOODS

Section 1(1) says any person who in the course of a trade or business:

    (a) applies a false trade description to any goods; or
    (b) supplies or offers to supply any goods to which a false trade description is applied shall be guilty of an offence.

Section 1 is a strict liability offence, *i.e.* no *mens rea* is required.

Section 2 sets out a list of 10 ways in which a trade description can be applied, *e.g.* if a can is described as containing 200 grams and only 50 grams are inside, there would be a breach of section 2(1)(a).

If a sweater is described as 100 per cent wool and it is in fact 50 per cent acrylic and 50 per cent cotton there would be a breach of section 2(1)(c).

The most common offences are committed in relation to the "clocking" of cars. Car complaints still form the bulk part of the complaints dealt with by the Office of Fair Trading (see OFT Annual Report, 2002) and lead to more convictions and compensation orders being made than in any other area. Turning back the mileometer on cars is capable of being a false trade description under section 2(1)(j): *R. v Hammerton Cars Ltd* (1976).

Punishment

Although most convictions result in a fine (the maximum for summary conviction per offence is £5,000), cases have made it clear, particularly in the clocking cases as outlined above, that car dealers who persistently clock cars could find themselves subject to a prison sentence (*R. v Hewitt, The Times*, 1991).

In the course of a business

The offence is only committed by someone acting in the course of a business. Private individuals are not "caught" by the Act. (But see section 23, the by-pass provision that could result in a conviction.)

"In the course of a business" was considered in the case of *Davies v Sumner* [1984] HL, where a self-employed courier part-exchanged his car that had an odometer reading of 18,100 when it had in fact covered 118,000.

When the defendant sold the car to the garage, was he acting in the course of a trade or business? The House of Lords decided not, as the sale was not an integral part of the business (the defendant was not in the car business, previously he had leased cars and was not involved in a regular practice of exchanging cars). It was merely incidental to the carrying on of the business.

In *Devlin v Hall* (1990) the *first sale* by a proprietor of a taxi firm of one of his two cars could not be said to amount to a normal regular practice and was therefore not done in the course of a business.

On the other hand, in *Havering London Borough v Stevenson* (1970), the defendant ran a car-hire business but intermittently sold cars from the forecourt. Although this was not his main business, and he was not a car dealer, the courts held he was acting in the course of a business as there was a practice of selling off cars.

Professions fall within the scope of the Act. See *Roberts v Leonard* (1995) where the defendant was a veterinary surgeon. The judge said he saw no sufficient reason why professionals should be excluded.

[**Note:** the Act applies to an offer to supply, section 6 and not just where the goods have actually been supplied. This covers the invitation to treat point in *Pharmaceutical Society of Great Britain v Boots Cash Chemists* (1952). The Divisional Court has also held that when goods had been defectively repaired and then returned to their owner, the return of the goods constituted a supply of goods for the purpose of section 1(1) of the Act. If the work had not been carried out as stated, then an offence of applying a false trade description had been committed *Formula One Autocentres Ltd v Birmingham City Council* (1998).]

What about disclaimer notices?

What better way to avoid liability than to try and disclaim. Can this be done under the Act? This device has been used particularly in the car clocking cases. It can be effective, but is subject to many restrictions:

(a) In order to be effective, the disclaimer must be introduced before the trader supplies the goods.

In *Norman v Bennett* (1974), it was stated that "the disclaimer must be as bold, precise and compelling as the trade description itself and must equal the trade description in the extent to which it is likely to get home to anyone interested in receiving the goods". In other words, the mileometer reading has to be made meaningless. Sentences in small print will not protect dealers, and general notices would appear to be ineffective. Notices must be displayed prominently.

See: *Zawadski v Sleigh* (1975);
London Borough of Waltham v T. G. Wheatley (1978);
London Borough of Ealing v Taylor (1995);
R. v Bull (1995).

(b) [**Note:** the difference between a car dealer who sells a "clocked" car and one who actually clocks the car himself.]

Newman v Hackney (1982) states that if the dealer is found to have clocked the car himself, then the disclaimer doctrine is not available.

The doctrine is therefore only available to someone who has *not* clocked the car.

However, where a motor dealer knew or had reasonable grounds for believing that the mileage travelled by a vehicle substantially exceeded that shown on the odometer, he could not effectively disclaim the reading merely by stating it was incorrect if he did not go on to reveal the truth as he knew it. (*Farrand v Lyndy Lazarus* (2002).) Therefore, a car dealer cannot nowadays close his eyes to the very obvious and claim the protection of a disclaimer notice.

There is a Code of Practice for motor dealers. No particular form of disclaimer is used, but the code states:

(a) the need to verify the recorded mileage with previous owners; and
(b) that any disclaimer used must be as bold and precise and compelling as the car's mileage reading itself and be effectively brought to the prospective customer's attention.

The government has introduced a voluntary scheme for recording mileage information when the annual road fund licence is renewed. However, consumer organisations are lobbying for a stricter form of control in an effort to reduce the practice of second hand car clocking.

Disclaimers in other areas

The case of *Kent County Council v Price* (1994) has raised problems for Trading Standards Officers in relation to counterfeit goods. A market trader put a notice on his stall saying "brand copies". He was selling T-shirts bearing brand names like "Levi" and "Adidas". The Divisional Court agreed this disclaimer was sufficient to escape conviction under the Trade Descriptions Act. Trading Standards Departments have expressed great concern at this case (see ITSA Press Release MPW/EDD/180693) but have said that although prosecutions will not work under the Trade Descriptions Act, they will use other legislation, *e.g.* Trade Marks Act 1994 or Copyright Designs and Patents Act 1988 to obtain a conviction. These statutes have now been amended by the Copyright, etc. and

Trade Marks (Offences and Enforcement) Act 2002. See, *e.g. R. v Torbay District Council, ex parte Singh* (1999) where the defendant was successfully convicted under the Trade Marks Act 1994. Note also *R. v Simon Wallace Keane* (2000) where again the defendant was successfully prosecuted under the Trade Marks Act. In *Lewin v Fuell* (1991), however, the Divisional Court had to consider whether an oral disclaimer in relation to watches, which were offered for supply bearing names such as "Cartier" and "Rolex" could be effective in nullifying the false trade descriptions. The court ruled that the offence was committed when the goods were exposed for supply and as the disclaimer came after the offence had been committed, it was too late to be effective. The prosecution was therefore successful using the Trade Descriptions Act.

Although defences will be discussed later, it is worth noting one particular detail at this point in relation to disclaimers. One defence under section 24 is that the defendant had taken all reasonable precautions and exercised all due diligence to avoid the commission of an offence. In *Simmons v Potter* (1975) it was held that because the defendant car dealers had not used a disclaimer notice, they had not exercised all reasonable precautions. They were therefore guilty of committing an offence.

Services

Section 14 of the Trade Descriptions Act relates to services. The difference between section 1 relating to goods and section 14 is that an element of *mens rea* is required. Section 14 states:

> "it shall be an offence for any person *in the course of any trade or business* (so what was said in relation to section 1 applies here) to make a statement which *he knows* to be false or *recklessly* to make a statement which is false as to services, accommodation or facilities".

This section will be considered with particular reference to holidays. These are the most likely kinds of service to occur in examinations and the most common service complaint to arise in practice.

Points to note:

(1) *Mens rea* is required. The defendant must knowingly or recklessly make a false statement: *MFI Warehouses v Nattrass* (1973), *Wings Ltd v Ellis* (1984), *Airtours v Shipley* (1994).

(2) A statement of intention relating to *a future* promise that is unfulfilled will not be a false trade description. *Beckett v Cohen* [1973]. Therefore, artists' impressions of hotels in holiday brochures, stating that the hotel "will be open in time for the next summer season" or "will have. . ." will not give rise to successful actions under the Act. (Although there may be liability under the civil law.)

(3) **Note:** however, if the description *implies* the *facility is in existence* then it may be actionable: *R. v Clarksons Holidays* (1972). If the promise can be construed as an implied statement of *present* intention, again a conviction may be obtained, *e.g. British Airways v Taylor* (1974) (airline over-booking), *R. v Avro plc* (1993) (tickets issued by flight-only operator, the return flight did not exist).

(4) If the facility existed at the moment the statement was made, but has broken down subsequently, then there will not normally be liability under the Act: *Sunair v Dodds* (1970).

So that, if a hotel is advertised as having air-conditioning or satellite TV and this breaks down whilst the consumer is at the hotel, there will be no liability under the Trade Descriptions Act (although again there may be liability under the civil law).

(5) What if the facility has never existed at all? In *Wings v Ellis* (1984), the respondents published a brochure that, *inter alia,* gave details of a holiday hotel in Sri Lanka. The hotel was stated as being fully air-conditioned. The hotel did not in fact have air-conditioning. The second edition of the tour brochure corrected the error and instructions were given out to travel agents. Mr X obtained a first edition of the brochure, was never given the correct information and booked the holiday. Wings were charged under section 14(1)(a) and were convicted. Although they had no desire to mislead the consumer, the simple question to be asked was did they know the statement was false at the time when it was made and the clear answer to this was yes, with reference to the *mens rea* required. See also *R. v Avro plc* (1993).

(6) The Act can give rise to multiple prosecutions as an offence can be committed every time the description is published: *R. v Thomson Holidays Ltd* (1974).

(7) "Money-back guarantees". In *James Ashley v London Borough of Sutton* (1995), a book was sold which promised success on the football pools and came with a money-back

guarantee. The guarantee was not honoured. The court said that customers who paid an inflated price for the book were in fact not buying goods but a service. The promise to refund had been broken and the defendant was liable under section 14. However, in *Dixon v Roberts* (1984) the court ruled that a price pledge promise to refund if the goods could be purchased cheaper elsewhere was not a service and the defendant was not liable under section 14. Price pledge promises nowadays are dealt with by the misleading prices legislation. See below, Chapter 15.

(8) What if the defendant tries to make matters right? Can this "cancel" out the offence? In *Cowburn v Focus* (1983), the defendant company ran a promotional offer, stating that 20 films could be hired free when a consumer rented a TV. This offer in fact expired a week earlier but the offer placards remained prominently displayed in the shop window. This 20 free films offer had been replaced by an offer for 6 free films. When the consumer rented the TV set he was asked for £1.50 towards postage and packing. As soon as he complained he was sent a refund of £1.50 and a voucher for 20 films. However, Trading Standards prosecuted and a successful conviction was obtained.

HOLIDAYS

At this stage, before we leave trade descriptions, in the light of the fact that holiday questions crop up with regularity in consumer law examinations, it is worth noting certain matters:

(1) In every holiday question look and see whether there is possible criminal liability under the Trade Descriptions Act 1968. This could result in a compensation order for the aggrieved individual without the necessity of pursuing individual civil actions.

(2) 1992 saw the introduction of the Package Travel Package Holidays and Package Tours Regulations 1992. These regulations result from European Directive 90/314 and are enacted under S.I. 1992/3288 as amended.

The regulations are nowadays the best way an aggrieved package holidaymaker can hope to achieve satisfaction. The regulations create both civil and criminal liability and apply to packages sold in the U.K. on or after December 31, 1992. Basically, a qualifying package must have been pre-arranged at an inclusive price and cover over 24 hours or include overnight accommodation. Regulation 2 contains definitions and refers to terms such as organiser and retailer rather than tour operator and travel agent. Business and conference travel could be covered under the regulations as the definition of consumer is wide enough to embrace them.

Regulation 4 creates implied terms for civil liability. Package organisers or retailers shall not supply any descriptive matter concerning the package which mislead the consumer. If they do, they will be liable to compensate the consumer for any loss that the consumer suffers in consequence. See, *e.g. Moore v Thomson Holidays* (1998).

Other regulations set out what information should be given to consumers before the contract is concluded and before the package commences. Included in Regulation 15 is a term that the organiser and/or retailer should be strictly liable for the proper performance of the obligations under the contract whether or not they are providing the service or whether such services are to be provided by other suppliers. See, *e.g. Wong Mee Wan v Kwan Kin Travel Services* (1995) and *Brannan v Airtours* (1999). Note for a successful claim under Regulation 15, the holidaymaker must show that the service provider was at fault.

In the following three cases, no fault could be proven. *Jones v Sunworld Ltd* (2003), *Singh v Libra Holidays* (2003), *Hone v Going Places Ltd* (2001). Once fault has been proven, then the tour operator is liable.

There are also terms involving security for refunds of money and for repatriation of the consumer in the event of insolvency.

The Department of Trade and Industry has published useful question and answer guidance booklets to the regulations that students will find most useful.

(3) When a consumer books a holiday on behalf of himself and his family it does appear that contractually any aggrieved party member can sue on the basis of agency. *Jackson v Horizon Holidays* (1975). This doctrine still appears to be true as far as holidays are concerned, in spite of what was said in *Woodar Investment Development Ltd v Wimpey Construction* (1980). In any event, the Package Travel Regulations define a consumer in such a way that members of a family and other party members are included.

(4) Also, under the civil law a holiday is a service. It cannot be split into component parts, so if something goes wrong it will give rise to—

    (a) a breach of section 13 of the Supply of Goods and Services Act (*Best v Wilson Travel* (1993)) also (*Wong Mee Wan v Kwan Kin Travel Services* (1995)) or, more likely;

    (b) a breach of contract, as an express term has been breached (consumers generally book with very precise terms as regards holiday accommodation so it is easier to sue for a breach of express terms);

    (c) an action in misrepresentation;

    (d) however, most importantly, where the holiday is a package, then the 1992 Regulations should be used.

(5) Damages for distress and disappointment are often awarded in holiday cases. Again, this doctrine appears to have survived in the holiday cases despite the more restrictive approach taken in *Hayes v Dodd* (1990). In the leading case of *Jarvis v Swan Tours* (1973), the total cost of the holiday was £63.45. The holiday was a disaster and the amount awarded, including distress and disappointment, was £125.

(6) In order to gain maximum benefit from the special damages rules in *Hadley v Baxendale* (1854), if there is a special request or problem, make sure the consumer notes this in writing to the tour operator. In *Kemp v Intasun* (1987) a casual conversation with the travel agent, by a consumer regarding her husband's asthmatic condition, did not have contractual consequences for the operator.

(7) As well as pursuing civil actions through the courts, a consumer may instead decide to pursue the claim via arbitration through ABTA (the Association of British Travel Agents). There is no mandatory obligation placed on the consumer to use this service, but it is an option to be considered. The case is heard on a documents-only basis, with none of the parties appearing to argue the case.

(8) Legislation has also been enacted in relation to timeshares, notably the Timeshare Act 1992 and the 1997 Timeshare Regulations. The 1992 Act gives consumers buying under United Kingdom law protection with the right to a 14-day cooling-off period and the Timeshare Regulations give additional rights to buyers throughout

the European Union. The 1992 Act has been amended to include these additional rights which involve brochure and contract requirements and the cancellation of any associated credit agreement or credit card payment if the timeshare contract is cancelled. The 1992 Act also imposes criminal liability on a timeshare seller who fails to comply with the requirements of the Act with fines of up to £5,000 on summary conviction. Unscrupulous sellers have attempted to circumvent the stringent regulation of time-shares by enticing consumers to join "Holiday Clubs" that are not regulated. The Office of Fair Trading has expressed concern about the activities of certain bogus holiday clubs but at present there are no plans for new legislation although consumer organisations are lobbying for this.

Defences to a Trade Descriptions Act claim

To return to trade descriptions, some defences will now be considered. It should be noted that the due diligence defence in particular is also of relevance in relation to food safety, misleading prices and product liability. Some principles of general application are set out below.

Section 24 of the Trade Descriptions Act states:

"It shall be a defence for the person charged to prove:
  (a) that the commission of the offence was due to a mistake, or to reliance on information supplied to him, or to the act or default of another person, an accident, or some other cause beyond his control; and
  (b) that he took all reasonable precautions and exercised all due diligence to avoid the commission of such an offence by himself or any person under his control."

Cars and the disclaimer doctrine have been considered earlier but it should be noted that an oral disclaimer would not be a defence under section 24 as reasonable precautions would at least have included a written disclaimer alongside the false trade description (*Lewin v Fuell* (1991)).

The various parts in (a) are separate and distinct. If mistake is pleaded, the mistake must be of the person charged, and no-one else. A corporate offender will not be able to rely on the mistake of one of its employees. *Birkenhead and District Co-operative Society v Roberts* (1970).

Act or default of another person

The case of *Tesco Supermarkets v Nattrass* (1972), which has caused immense difficulties in practice, established that insofar as a company is concerned, its employees are "another person" allowing the defence to be successfully pleaded. Only executive members for example, a director, will be classed as the company. However, both limbs must be satisfied, so in *Haringey v Piro Shoes* (1976), although the offence was due to the act or default of another, not all reasonable precautions nor all due diligence had been exercised. In *Gale v Dixon Store Group* (1994) the defendants supplied as new a computer that had previously been returned by another customer as defective. An offence was committed under section 1. The defendants sought to rely on the statutory defence but as in the *Haringey* case, they also had to show that they had taken all reasonable precautions and exercised all due diligence. There was no evidence of any generally applicable system before the incident to prevent such a problem although a procedure was introduced after the event. Because there was no procedure in force at the time of the offence, Dixons could not avail themselves of the section 24 defence. However, in *Asda Stores Ltd v Birmingham City Council* (1998) (a case brought under the Consumer Protection Act on misleading pricing), the due diligence defence and act or default of another succeeded. The defence also succeeded in *Lincolnshire County Council v Safeway Stores plc* (1999) (a case brought under the Food Safety Act 1990) and in *Tesco Stores Ltd v Norfolk County Council* (2001) (a case brought under the Children and Young Persons Act 1933 for selling cigarettes to a child under 16).

Sampling and testing in relation to due diligence

Can suppliers dealing with large quantities of goods rely on sampling to show they have exercised all due diligence and taken all reasonable precautions? This is a difficult area and every case will have to be decided on a question of fact, but in *Rotherham Metropolitan BC v Raysun (U.K.) Ltd* (1988) the defendants imported 100,000 packets of children's crayons per annum. The Hong Kong agents were supposed to analyse samples and send back any adverse reports. None was ever received. A single packet was tested in England. The crayons were described as poisonless, whereas they contained an excessive amount of toxic material. The defendants were convicted as they had not taken all reasonable precautions. See *Hurley v Martinez and Co. Ltd* (1991). (Supplier again acting on assurances given further up the chain of supply without independent verification.) *Held:* in this instance the defence was made out. In *Harrow London Borough Council v W H Smith Trading Ltd* (2001) the defence was made out by the defendants when they were prosecuted for selling a magazine with a CD ROM without a classification certificate contrary to section 14A of the Video Recordings Act 1984. The defendants were under no obligation to carry out independent checks on their supplier whom they had traded with for the previous 20 years. However, in *P & M Supplies Essex Ltd v Devon County Council* (1991) the Divisional Court said that the burden was on the defendants themselves to show that their testing system was adequate for both the type and number of goods involved and that this system was carried out scrupulously. On the facts this time, the defence was not made out. See also *Dudley Metropolitan Council v Roy Firman Ltd* (1992) and *London Borough of Ealing v Taylor* (1995).

13. UNSAFE GOODS

When the consumer has a contract, there are rights under section 14 of the Sale of Goods Act or equivalent statutes against the retailer and under the Consumer Protection Act against the manufacturer. Where there is no contract at all, the consumer will still have civil rights under the Consumer Protection Act. If the consumer is successful, then he will recover compensation.

In this chapter criminal liability for unsafe goods will be considered. The Department of Trade and Industry has for many years operated a Consumer Safety Unit. The statistics on injuries caused by defective products prove grim reading at times. The main legislation imposing criminal sanctions on producers and suppliers of unsafe consumer goods is currently the General Product Safety Regulations 1994 which have largely replaced the criminal liability imposed by the Consumer Protection Act 1987, Pt II. At present, the Department of Trade and Industry is reviewing the 1994 Regulations with new regulations anticipated in 2004. These will extend the definition of product and will cover products that were originally designed for use by trained professionals but have now migrated to be used by untrained consumers. (*e.g.* DIY power tools). Powers of recall are to be improved and penalties increased in line with other Health and Safety legislation. Set out next is the current position with regard to product safety.

GENERAL PRODUCT SAFETY REGULATIONS 1994

The General Product Safety Regulations came into force as a result of a European Community Directive. This legislation intends to fill the gaps in European safety legislation by stating that:

   (a) all products supplied to consumers must be safe. This applies whether the consumer paid for them or whether they were supplied free;

   (b) safe products are defined; and

   (c) a framework for assessing safety is set out.

[**Note:**

   (a) The regulations apply to products but do not apply to service activities.

   (b) New and second hand products are covered but not second hand products classed as antiques. Generally, products supplied for repair or reconditioning before use, provided the supplier informs the consumer to this effect are also excluded. However, some second hand products, *e.g.* electrical and gas cookers and heaters may be subject to other regulations made under the 1987 Act so that they can be supplied to a person carrying on a business repairing or reconditioning such goods or sold as scrap but cannot be sold to consumers for repair or reconditioning.

   (c) Products are best described according to the regulations as goods supplied to consumers for their private use. (Regulation 2(1).)

   (d) Only products supplied in the course of a commercial activity are covered, therefore private sellers are not subject to these regulations.

   (e) If a product is covered by a specific product directive, *e.g.* a toy, then the directive rather than the General Product Safety Regulations will apply.]

What is a safe product?

A safe product is any product, which under normal or reasonably foreseeable conditions of use, presents no risk or only the minimum risk compatible with the product's use and which is consistent with a high level of protection for consumers. The safety of a product will be assessed under Regulation 2(1) having regard to a number of matters including packaging, instructions for assembly and maintenance, labelling, what characteristics the product possesses, and whether children will be expected to use it.

[**Note:** goods do not have to be absolutely safe but the risks must be reduced to the minimum. The regulations are concerned with unsafe goods and not shoddy products.]

Suppliers covered by the regulations

The regulations apply to all persons in the business supply chain and therefore include manufacturers, importers, wholesalers and retailers, see *Padgett Brothers (A to Z) Ltd v Coventry City Council* (1998) where the defendant was the importer of Chinese hammers and was successfully convicted under the regulations. Suppliers are then categorised into whether they are producers or distributors. A producer is the manufacturer or someone who holds himself out as a manufacturer whereas a distributor is someone in the supply chain whose activities do not affect the safety of a product.

Responsibilities of producers and distributors

(a) They both have responsibilities to supply only products that are safe and if necessary to provide consumers with warnings and to inform of risks.

(b) Producers have a primary duty under Regulation 7 to place only safe products on the market. They have to provide information to enable consumers to use the product in a safe way to avoid risks, *e.g.* by wearing gloves. Monitoring and sample testing may be appropriate.

(c) A distributor is required under Regulation 9 to act with due care to help ensure the products supplied are safe. He must not supply products that he knows, or should have presumed on the basis of the information in his possession, to be dangerous. Under these regulations, retailers will therefore be able to use similar defences to the defences that existed under the old legislation.

Defences under the regulations

(a) The regulations provide for a due diligence defence under Regulation 14(1). This will allow a producer or distributor to show that he took all reasonable steps and exercised all due diligence to avoid the commission of an offence.
(b) It is also a defence to show successfully that the offence was due to the act or default of another or due to reliance on information supplied by another person although these are subject to taking reasonable steps to prevent the commission of an offence.

Enforcement

The regulations make provision for enforcement. Regulation 11 provides for enforcement authorities and sets out the powers of those authorities. These include powers to issue suspension notices and to obtain information.

Penalties

The current penalties on summary conviction are a fine of up to £5,000 or a prison term of up to three months or both. The regulations only give rise to criminal liability and do not involve civil liability.

The Department of Trade and Industry have published a very useful guidance leaflet on the 1994 Regulations, entitled the "General Product Safety Regulations 1994, Guidance for Businesses, Consumers and Enforcement Authorities".

14. FOOD SAFETY

In recent years there has been a massive increase in reported cases involving food poisoning. According to figures put out by the Department of Environmental Health, the number is steadily rising year by year. The public has become acutely aware of problems relating to food safety with the BSE and CJD food scares and most recently the media attention that has been focused on genetically modified food. These particular food safety problems have resulted in an enormous amount of new food legislation and food labelling regulations. The government has also set up the Food Standards Agency.

The aim of this chapter is, however, confined to consider the effect of the 1990 Food Safety Act and how this act can assist consumers. In 1990 the Food Safety Act came into being. This aims "to control all aspects of food safety throughout the food distribution chain, from the plough to the plate".

It should be noted that breaches of the Food Safety Act give rise to *criminal* liability only. (Remember, under the Sale of Goods Act an injured person can sue for a breach of section 14 and add their injury claims on as a direct consequence of the breach. The Consumer Protection Act 1987 could also be used to obtain compensation against a manufacturer.) A breach of the Food Safety Act will however assist a consumer in achieving compensation under the civil law.

Penalties

On indictment there is an unlimited fine and/or imprisonment for a maximum of two years. On summary conviction there is an upper limit fine of £20,000 for breaches of section 7, section 8 and section 14. For other breaches there are fines of up to £5,000 and imprisonment for a maximum of six months.

The offences

There are four major offences that students should know and appreciate, apart from many others contained in the Act. These are the provisions contained in sections 7, 8, 14 and 15. First of all the definition of food should be noted. This is partly defined by section 1(1). A second list of items are excluded in section 1(2).

Included in the definition are:

(a) Drinks (including bottled mineral water) but NOT the supply of water to premises (governed by the Water Act).

[**Note:** that the supply of water to the tap is governed by the various Water Acts, but that once the water has left the tap it is regulated by the Food Safety Act.]

(b). Additives. Section 1(1)(b).
(c) Chewing Gum.

There are also sections governing contact materials (*i.e.* crockery, cutlery, plastic wrapping, etc.).

Excluded are:

(a) live animals;
(b) animal foodstuffs; and
(c) controlled drugs and medicines.

Rendering food injurious to health

Section 7 creates a specific offence of rendering food "injurious to health with the intent that it should be sold for human consumption".

According to section 7 the offence can be committed in four ways:

s.7.1(a) by adding any article or substance to the food;
s.7.1(b) by using any article or substance as an ingredient in the preparation of the food;
s.7.1(c) abstracting any constituent from the food; or
s.7.1(d) subjecting the food to any other process or treatment.

Section 3 of the Act states a presumption that if food commonly used for human consumption is sold, the sale is for human consumption.

There is one loophole left in section 7, *i.e.* that no offence is committed by someone who *fails* to subject food to a necessary process or treatment. However, a successful prosecution should be available under section 8.

Selling food not complying with food safety requirements

Section 8 creates a number of offences. It says:

> "Any person who sells for human consumption or offers exposes or advertises for sale for such consumption or has in his possession for the purpose of such sale or of preparation for such sale any food which fails to comply with food safety requirements shall be guilty of an offence."

The offence in section 8 can only be committed if:

(a) food is rendered injurious to health under section 7;
(b) it is unfit for human consumption; or
(c) it is so contaminated that it would not be reasonable to expect it to be used for human consumption. Under previous legislation, it has been held that a person can be convicted of an offence of selling food, even though the end result substance sold is not food at all. What is necessary is that it should be sold *as food*.

In *Meah v Roberts* (1978) the defendant mistakenly supplied caustic soda instead of lemonade. He was convicted of an offence.

[Note that the loophole mentioned earlier in relation to section 7 (*i.e.* a failure to do something) could result in an acquittal under section 8(2)(a) as there has been no offence committed. BUT, if the failure results in the food being unfit for human consumption, then an offence will have been committed under section 8(2)(b) so failure to act can lead to a successful prosecution.]

What is meant by unfit for human consumption?

It should be noted that food can be unfit for human consumption even if it poses no health hazard. *David Greig v Goldfinch* (1961)—this involved a pork pie found to be developing black mould under the crust. This was discovered to be a harmless bacteria. However, the justices fortunately found that the food was unfit for human consumption.

There had been difficulties in earlier cases when extras had been found in food, *e.g.* string in a loaf of bread: *Turner v Owen* [1956] 1 Q.B. 48, or metal in a cream bun: *J. Miller v Battersea* (1956). Arguments had been successfully put forward that these extras did not make food unfit for human consumption. Nowadays, the defendants should merely be charged under section 8(2)(c), *i.e.* supplying contaminated food. In *R. v F. & M. Dobson* (1995) where a knife blade was found in chocolate confectionery, the defendants were convicted of supplying food unfit for human consumption under section 8(2)(c) and were fined £7,000.

Foods which mislead consumers

Sections 14 and 15 of the Act will now be considered. The aim of these sections is to prevent consumers from being misled and to try to make sure that they obtain food "of the appropriate nature, substance and quality demanded" (already students should be thinking of the civil law under the Sale of Goods Act 1979, sections 13 and 14).

Section 14 of the Food Safety Act states that any person who sells to a purchaser's prejudice any food that is not of the nature or substance or quality demanded by the purchaser shall be guilty of an offence. Thus, anyone who sells goods that do not correspond with their description, could be guilty of an offence under section 14. In *McDonald's Hamburgers v Windle* (1987) the product requested was Diet McDonald's Cola. Ordinary cola was served. An offence was committed. In recent years, the pizza chain, Pizza Hut, were fined under this section for supplying a pizza which contained a chicken topping when a vegetarian pizza had been ordered.

This section may also be used where regulations prescribe that certain products can only be sold as mince, for example, when they contain not more than a certain percentage of fat. When regulatory standards are set down, food must comply with these standards in order to be of the substance demanded, *e.g.* fish cakes under the Food Standards Fish Cakes Order 1950 mean that to describe goods as a fish cake the fish cake has to have a 35 per cent minimum fish content. As well as the general offence of falsely or misleadingly describing or presenting food, there are also detailed regulations relating to food labelling and, more recently, regulations relating to foods that contain genetically modified materials.

Section 15 of the Act says any person who gives with any food sold by him . . . a label . . . which falsely describes the food or is likely to mislead as to the nature or substance or qualify of the food shall be guilty of an offence.

Again, there could be an overlap between sections 14 and 15.

[**Note:** the wording is "LIKELY TO MISLEAD", no-one need actually be misled.]

Thus, these are the sections most likely to occur in examination questions. The statute also contains many powers for Food Inspectors to inspect and seize food (section 9) and to issue notices including powers to close down premises. These questions are not usually examined in depth on consumer law papers, but students should examine their particular syllabus and revise accordingly and make use of the many detailed works now appearing in this area. New food hygiene regulations have been introduced as well as many orders from the European Community in respect of food products.

Defences

Like most consumer protection statutes, the Food Safety Act does provide defences in certain situations, notably the due diligence defence contained in section 21(1). See *Lincolnshire County Council v Safeway Stores plc* (1999). This defence is discussed in more detail in the section on trade descriptions and broadly speaking most of the principles can be transferred to the Food Safety legislation. For further information in this area students should again consult the detailed guides to the Act.

---

15. MISLEADING PRICES

For some decades now, there has been legislation to try to curb misleading prices and bargain offers. See, for instance, section 11 of the Trade Descriptions Act 1968.

There is nothing more galling, as far as a consumer is concerned, than to think they have grabbed a bargain only to discover when they reach the cash desk that they are asked for extra money. From a civil point of view, all law students are of course familiar with the famous decision in *Pharmaceutical Society of Great Britain v Boots Cash Chemists* (1952). When consumers take their goods to the checkouts they are merely making an offer to purchase. The store, when displaying the goods, is making an invitation to treat. So, when Mrs Bloggs takes her £5 bargain blouse to the cash desk and is asked for £15, under the civil law there is nothing she can do. Her offer of £5 has been rejected.

The latest attempt to control prices is now contained in Part III of the Consumer Protection Act 1987. This replaces section 11 of the Trade Descriptions Act and the Price Marking (Bargain Offers) Orders 1979.

The criminal offence of misleading consumers

The Act makes it a criminal offence to give consumers a misleading price indication about goods, services, or accommodation (including the sale of new homes). However, the Act only creates a general offence, it then empowers the Secretary of

State to approve a code of practice setting out guidance for retailers as to the practices they ought to follow. This Code of Practice is currently under review by the Department of Trade and Industry and changes are anticipated in the near future.

The Code of Practice

The important factor to note is that the Act does not require a retailer to do as the Code states. As long as the price indication is not misleading, there will be no criminal offence. On the other hand, even if the Code is complied with, if the price is misleading, then the retailer could be guilty of an offence. This situation is extremely unlikely to occur.

The important factor is therefore that it is only a Code. The retail industry are seeking to put their house in order by self-regulation and the Secretary of State at present, has agreed to this state of affairs.

What is misleading?

Misleading is defined in section 21 of the Act and covers indications about any conditions attached to a price, about future prices, price comparisons, as well as indications about the actual price the consumer will have to pay.

Enforcement

The Act is enforced by Local Trading Standards Officers. The Act provides for a defence of due diligence as in other consumer criminal statutes. Obviously, as stated earlier, failure to follow the Code may make it difficult to show this defence.

The Code

The following guidance, *inter alia*, is given to retailers in the Code.

Price comparisons

(a) Paragraph 1.1.2—says the higher price as well as the price the retailer intends to charge should always be stated. Therefore, £10 reduced to £5 is good, but SALE PRICE £6 is misleading.

(b) Paragraph 1.2.1—says that in any comparison between the present selling price and another price, the previous price as well as the new lower price should be stated. Thus, "Blouse—£10, our normal price £20" complies with the Code.

(c) Following on from section 11 of the Trade Descriptions Act, in para. 1.2.2 the Code states the product should have been available to consumers for at least 28 consecutive days in the last 6 months and in the same shop where the reduced price is being offered. If not, then this should be made clear. This is why notices appear in shops under the heading of Consumer Protection Act—"The goods sold below were previously offered at our Outer Hebrides Branch between 14–16 January at £50—Price Today £10". If no notice had been put up, the £10 notice would have contravened the Code.

(d) Paragraph 1.2.3—general disclaimers should not be used but specific stores and prices should be referred to.

(e) Paragraph 1.2.6—in the Code it is stated that if a series of reductions is made then the highest price, the intervening price and the current selling price should be shown, *e.g.* £10, £5 NOW ONLY £2.50. A leading chain store advertises during the sale period: "£25 NOW £2.50. During the last three weeks these goods have been subject to a series of reductions. Further details on these reductions can be obtained from our Head Office." It is a matter of conjecture as to whether this satisfies the Code.

Introductory offers

(a) Paragraph 1.3.1—states that an introductory offer should not be described as such unless it is intended to charge a higher price later.

(b) Paragraph 1.3.2—states that an introductory offer should not be allowed to run overlong, but does not state how long this period should be. The word reasonable is quoted.

(c) Paragraph 1.3.4—future increased prices can be quoted, *e.g.* "Our price now until June 10—£180. After Sales Price—£250." This has become a favourite with the furniture retailing industry.

Comparison with prices related to different circumstances

There are a number of guidelines here. Again the most common to be met in practice are:

(a) for goods in a totally different state, *e.g.* "price in a kit from £50, ready assembled £100";

(b) reductions for pensioners on certain days. These must be expressed in such a way that consumers are not misled and the goods or services must be available at the higher price. See paragraphs 1.4.3 and 1.4.4.

References to worth or value

(a) Paragraph 1.8.1—states do not compare prices with slogans such as worth or value. If goods are advertised as worth £50, it has to be shown they are actually available in the shops for £50. *MGN Ltd v Ritters* (1997). Note: price comparisons with another trader's actual prices are allowed and this is followed by a number of leading retailers in their advertising claims.

(b) The price pledge slogan "if you can buy for less we will refund the difference".

(c) Paragraph 1.5.2—states do not make statements like this about your own brand products unless your offer applies to another trader's equivalent goods. In a case under the Act, *R. v Warwickshire CC, ex parte Johnson* (1993) a price pledge promise stating "We will beat any TV Hi-Fi and Video price by £20 on the spot" was held to be misleading when the store failed to honour this promise. This case failed however as the prosecution had been brought against the store manager and should have been brought against the retail organisation concerned.

Actual price to the consumer

(a) Paragraph 2.1—this follows closely on from the Trade Descriptions Act and is the easiest to pursue in practice. The Act makes it an offence to indicate a price for goods or services which is lower than the one that actually applies. Therefore, in the example given in the beginning of this chapter, when Mrs Bloggs was asked for £15 for the blouse, a criminal offence may have been committed. However, where there is a discrepancy between the ticket price displayed on a shop item and the price disclosed by a bar code reader and the store cashier applies the lower ticket price then no offence is committed, *Toys "R" Us v Gloucestershire County Council* (1994). It is not necessary for the prosecution to produce an individual consumer who was misled by the price: *MFI Furniture Centres Ltd v Hibbert* (1995).

(b) Paragraphs 2.2.1–2.2.7—deal with extras such as delivery charges and postage and state these must be clearly advertised. See *Toyota (GB) Ltd v North Yorkshire County Council* (1998) where a bold headline indicated a car retail sale price of £11,665 but in very small print at the foot of the advertisement certain extra charges were set out. The Divisional Court held an offence had been committed, the car was not offered for sale at £11,665. Also all price indications to private consumers must include VAT.

The second offence

Finally, note, a second offence is created, *i.e.* a price indication that is correct when given but which later becomes misleading (section 20(2) of the Consumer Protection Act). This section was considered in *Thomson Tour Operations v Birch* (1999) when X, a holiday-maker, booked a holiday subject to a claim in the Thomson Company's Fair Trading Charter that "our early price promise means that if we reduce the total price of a holiday after you have booked it we will charge you the new lower price". When 10 per cent discounts were given to customers who booked at a later date it was held that Thomson had not committed an offence in respect of X's booking. For a case to succeed, it had to be established that, at the time of booking, X could expect the holiday price to be reduced and on the facts there was no evidence of this. The Code should be consulted for further guidance.

Defences

Section 39 creates a defence of due diligence similar to that set out in the Trade Descriptions Act. It states, "subject to the following provisions of this section, it shall be a defence for that person to show he took all reasonable steps, and exercised all due diligence to avoid committing the offence". See *Asda Stores v Birmingham City Council* (1998).

[**Note:** however, unlike section 24 of the Trade Descriptions Act, the defendant does not have to show that the offence was due to a number of specific reasons although in practice it is likely that the defendant will bring forward similar evidence.]

16. WAYS OF PURSUING RIGHTS

In a work of this kind, it is not possible to go through the civil court system to show how disappointed consumers can pursue their rights. Major changes have recently been made to all the rules of Civil Procedure putting in place the Woolf reforms, and of course the no win, no fee scheme under which legal firms can now operate, depending on the type of case involved.

However, it should be noted that as a large number of consumer claims involve amounts of less than £5,000 and as the issue of legal costs deters many litigants from going to court, one way of keeping costs down to a minimum is to commence an action through the small claims track section of the county court where the amount claimed is below £5,000.

The advantages of this system are:

(a) The claimant (and the defendant) are not, save in exceptional circumstances, responsible for the losing side's legal costs. Each side remains liable for their own costs and litigants are encouraged to represent themselves in a speedier and more informal atmosphere.

(b) There are fixed court costs on issuing proceedings. This cost is usually borne by the losing side.

(c) Following the Woolf reforms, the case is heard using the arbitration system and in most county courts before a district judge.

Many retailers also belong to Trade Associations, *e.g.* Society of Motor Manufacturers and Traders, and the Association may give assistance to consumers. There are also Codes of Practice governing various industries, *e.g.* ABTA governing the travel industry. Again, a consumer may choose to gain satisfaction using arbitration schemes operated by bodies such as ABTA.

Rather than use the court system, consumers cannot be forced to use an arbitration scheme as opposed to the court system. (Arbitration Act 1996).

Other ways of achieving consumer satisfaction

Many of the matters considered above involve the consumer in ultimately using the court system to gain redress. There are other ways of achieving consumer satisfaction that are considered here and although they may not gain individual personal satisfaction for an aggrieved consumer, the general public may be protected. The Enterprise Act 2002 has radically altered the way in which the Office of Fair Trading, the main Government Agency responsible for implementing consumer protection measures, operates. It has replaced the office of the Director-General of Fair Trading with a new statutory authority. It gives the Office of Fair Trading new powers to approve consumer codes of conduct.

One way of protecting consumers was by using Stop Now Orders. These came into effect in 2001 and allow the Office of Fair Trading to issue orders stopping unlawful behaviour that damages consumers. Breaching an order can lead to fines or imprisonment for contempt of court. They allow swifter action against a range of unfair trading practices set out in the legislation. The Enterprise Act, Part 8 has replaced the 2001 Stop Now Orders and extended them to cover more unfair practices. In addition, "Super-complaints" have been created and named consumer bodies have been empowered to make these complaints. The aim behind all this new legislation is to protect the public at large from unscrupulous traders and unfair trading methods. Part 8 gives no new civil rights to consumers. They will still have to seek individual redress through the courts. However, by using these new powers set out above consumer rights and awareness should be much improved.

17. EXAMINATION CHECKLIST

(1) State which consumer statute governs the transaction. This may be:
   (a) Sale of Goods Act 1979;
   (b) Supply of Goods (Implied Terms) Act 1973 for hire purchase transactions; or
   (c) Supply of Goods and Services Act 1982 for work and materials contracts, exchange contracts, hire contracts and services contracts.

(2) State the implied conditions that govern the contract, *i.e.* sections 13 and 14 of the Sale of Goods Act 1979 and their equivalents in the 1973 and 1982 Acts. Also relevant here is section 13 of the SGSA 1982 as regards services.

(3) Look at the effect of breach of condition.

(4) Is there an exclusion clause?

(5) Has it been incorporated into the contract by the common law rules?

(6) If it has been incorporated, look at the effect of the UCTA 1977 on the clause.

(7) This will involve a discussion of sections 6 and 7 of the UCTA (where implied conditions regarding goods are excluded), and a discussion of the phrase "dealing as a consumer".

(8) Where an attempt to exclude liability for services is made, this will involve a discussion of section 2 of the UCTA 1977 and where property damage only is concerned, then a discussion of the reasonableness test is required.

(9) All other exclusion clauses will be discussed under section 3 of the UCTA and again the reasonableness test must be discussed.

(10) Consider the effects of the Unfair Terms in Consumer Contracts Regulations 1999. If the clause is deemed to be unfair then it can be made void.

(11) Look at the effect of acceptance if it is a Sale of Goods Act contract, and affirmation if it is a 1973 or 1982 Act transaction.

[12] Consider the four additional remedies pursuing the route in the Sale of Goods Act as amended by 2002 Regulations.

(13) Look at the remedies for breach of contract and the rule in *Hadley v Baxendale*.

(14) Consider the credit aspects.

(15) State the basics of the Consumer Credit Act 1974.

(16) State clearly whether the transaction is hire purchase, conditional sale, loan, credit sale, credit card transaction, etc.

(17) If the transaction is one of hire purchase or conditional sale, then aside from the defective goods aspect, termination under sections 99 to 101 of the Consumer Credit Act 1974 will probably occur in the question.

(18) If it is a loan, then state whether it is a debtor-creditor or debtor-creditor-supplier agreement, giving reasons. If it is a three-party debtor-creditor-supplier agreement, *i.e.* a

loan-linked agreement or credit card transaction for the purchase of goods or services, then almost certainly a discussion of section 75 of the CCA on joint liability is required.

(19) Remember loan agreements cannot be terminated.

(20) All aspects of credit should be looked at under three headings:
  (i) How can I get out of the agreement?
  (ii) The goods are defective; and
  (iii) The debtor cannot afford to pay.

(21) For questions involving (20)(i), learn formalities, licensing, cancellation, withdrawal and termination.

(22) For questions involving (20)(ii), learn three basic statutes (*i.e.* 1979, 1973 and 1982 Acts) and sections 75 and 56 of the 1974 Consumer Credit Act.

(23) For questions involving (20)(iii), learn extortionate credit, termination (if H.P. or conditional sale of agreement), and time orders.

(24) Learn practically how to enforce the rights.

(25) Always respond to the facts of the question, *e.g.* if a default notice has been sent, respond to it, do not merely write out normal remedies.

(26) Note small claims and county court procedure.

(27) Other advice, such as contacting trade associations, manufacturers (note the Consumer Protection Act 1987).

(28) Arbitration.

(29) Compensation under the Trade Descriptions Act 1968.

---

18. SAMPLE QUESTIONS AND MODEL ANSWERS

QUESTION 1

Alan purchased a Seal car nine months ago from WonderCars Ltd on hire purchase terms financed by Grasping Finance Ltd for a total price of £12,800 including charges of £2,500 and a part exchange allowance of £2,000. The price was payable over three years in equal instalments. During the negotiations, WonderCar's Sales Manager stated that Seal were noted for their mechanical reliability and finish. However, the brakes, gear box and body work were defective on delivery. Alan returned the car a dozen times to the garage during the nine months, but the faults were never corrected.

(a) Advise Alan as to his rights and against whom they should be pursued.
(b) Advise Alan as to the options open to him if he calls 12 months after the purchase and tells you that he has been made redundant, cannot afford the repayments and is three months in arrears. Assume that there are no faults this time.

Answer

The first part of this question involves identifying the type of transaction concerned. Once this has been done then the contractual rights will be analysed and Alan can be advised as to his rights and remedies.

Alan has purchased his car on hire purchase terms. The transaction is therefore governed by Supply of Goods (Implied Terms) Act 1973. As the transaction is one of hire purchase, WonderCars will have sold the car to Grasping Finance Ltd who will hire the car out to Alan with an option to purchase. Contractually WonderCars "drop" out of the situation, and all of Alan's rights under the 1973 Act are exercised against Grasping Finance Ltd.

Under the Act, by section 10, where a person deals in the course of a business (as Grasping Finance Ltd do here), then there is an implied condition that:

(a) The goods will be of satisfactory quality. Satisfactory quality is defined in section 10(2B) of the 1973 Act. We are told that the brakes, gear box and bodywork were defective on delivery and that the faults still remain. It must be considered what are a buyer's expectations in relation to a new car. Clearly, the car must work mechanically but what about appearance defects? In *Rogers v Parish* (1987) the Court of Appeal said that a buyer not only expected a new car to function properly but that it should "look good". In *Bernstein v Pamson Motors* (1986) the engine of a new Nissan car seized up. The car was said not to be of merchantable quality. Today this car would not be of satisfactory quality. In this question, the faults would seem to be sufficiently serious to say that this condition has been breached and the goods are not of satisfactory quality. The definition of *satisfactory quality* now includes appearance defects.

Section 10 also states that the goods have to be reasonably fit for their purpose where the buyer relies on the skill and judgement of the seller. Where the buyer has "bought" from a reputable supplier, as here, then reliance can be implied: *Grant v Australian Knitting Mills* (1936). Clearly, it can be argued that a car which keeps breaking down is unfit for its purpose: *R&B Customs Brokers v UDT* (1988) and therefore there is a breach of this implied condition.

Section 9 of the 1973 Act states that the goods must comply with their description. The sales manager of WonderCars made certain claims regarding reliability and finish. It is likely that these claims will be regarded as mere sales talk and will not be terms of the contract.

However, there is a possibility that by using section 56 of the Consumer Credit Act which states that in any antecedent negotiations (as here where Alan discussed his purchase) then the supplier (Grasping Finance) is directly liable for any misrepresentations made by the credit broker (WonderCars). Clearly, depending on what was actually said, then a misrepresentation action could be considered.

The transaction concerned is one of hire purchase. There would appear to be a breach of condition of section 10 of the Supply of Goods (Implied) Terms Act 1973. This would entitle Alan to reject the goods, recover any monies paid and liability for future instalments would cease. In hire purchase transactions there is no doctrine of acceptance, only affirmation. (*Yeoman Credit v Apps* (1962); *Shine v General Guarantee Corp.* (1988)). Affirmation is a question of fact but on the grounds Alan has constantly complained about the car then he would not appear to have affirmed the contract (*Rogers v Parish* (1986)) unlike *Shine v General Guarantee Corp.* Alan should immediately notify the finance company telling them he is rejecting the car.

(b) Alan purchased the car under a regulated Consumer Credit Act agreement. This is because it is a hire purchase agreement of credit of less that £25,000 extended to an individual and is not exempt. If there are no faults with the car, and no possibility of cancellation of withdrawal then the only way out for Alan is to terminate the agreement. Under sections 99 and 100 of the Consumer Credit Act where there is a regulated hire purchase agreement (as here) Alan can terminate it as follows—

(i) he is liable for any arrears accrued due, *i.e.* £900 (£300 per month instalments);

(ii) he is liable to bring the payments up to half the total price, *i.e.* £6,400 less £2,000 less £2,700 paid. This leaves £1,700 (including arrears) to pay. The court has no discretion regarding the three months arrears of £900 but could award a lesser sum than the remaining £800 (unlikely here).

Therefore if Alan wishes to terminate it is a costly option and he has to hand back the goods.

If he wishes to keep the car, because he has already paid more than one-third the goods are protected and cannot be seized back without a court order (section 90 of the Consumer Credit Act). It might be in Alan's best interest to re-negotiate the instalment payments paying only what he can afford or wait until a default notice is served under section 87 of the Consumer Credit Act and then apply for a time order section 129 of the Consumer Credit Act. This gives a debtor more time to pay and as it is a hire purchase agreement the order can relate not only to arrears but also to future instalments. The answer therefore depends on whether Alan wishes to keep the car or to return it.

QUESTION 2

John seeks your advice in the following situation.

A week ago he decided to change his car. He went along to his usual garage, Wrecks Motors, where he saw a beautiful sports car. The proprietor, Mr Smith, told him it was a very economical car, fun and in excellent condition.

John decided to buy it on hire purchase terms. The cash price was £4,700 and Mr Smith allowed John £1,800 for his old car. John drove the sports car away and told the salesman to send all the necessary forms round to his office to sign.

The following day a salesman came round to the office, where John signed the HP forms with Royal Finance Ltd. The total HP price, including interest and life insurance premiums (which the finance company insisted John take out for three years) was £5,400, the car acting as deposit, leaving a balance of £3,600 to be paid by 36 monthly instalments of £100. John was given a copy of the agreement.

Unfortunately, John's wife detests the car: she took it out for a drive and, being unaccustomed to handling it, scraped it when trying to drive it into the garage. She then declared that she would never drive it and John must return the car. The damage will cost approximately £100 to put right.

John wants to know whether there is any way he can get out of the agreement without it costing him too much.

Answer

The agreement between John and Royal Finance is a regulated consumer credit agreement under the CCA 1974, being an agreement between an individual and a creditor who provides him with credit not exceeding £25,000 (section 8). It is not exempt. There is nothing to suggest that John's business is a company. It is a two-party restricted-use fixed-sum debtor-creditor-supplier agreement as it is HP (section 12(a)).

It is not clear from the facts whether the agreement became executed when John signed it. It would be executed if the salesman signed on the "occasion" (section 63(1)). If it was unexecuted there is a possibility that John could withdraw from the prospective agreement. However, notice of withdrawal must reach the other party before acceptance and, as acceptance is valid on posting, Royal Finance Ltd's acceptance might already be in the post by the time John's withdrawal arrives. (However, if John purported to withdraw but was too late it would be taken as notice of his cancellation in writing.)

It is a cancellable agreement under section 67 of the CCA 1974 because there were antecedent negotiations involving oral representations in the presence of the debtor (*i.e.* Smith was a credit broker conducting negotiations in relation to goods to be sold to the debtor within section 56(1) and he made statements relating to the car) and the agreement was signed away from the business premises of the creditor or negotiator. The agreement can therefore be cancelled by John serving notice of cancellation by the end of the fifth day following the day he received his second copy or notice of cancellation rights (section 68). If the agreement was unexecuted, John must be sent a copy of the executed agreement within seven days of making the agreement (*i.e.* acceptance). If it was executed he must be sent a notice of his cancellation rights within seven days of the agreement being made (section 64).

As it is only six days since he signed and as either a second copy or notice must be sent by post in the case of a cancellable agreement (sections 63(3) and 64(1)(b)), he should be entitled to cancel in either case.

John may cancel by serving a notice in writing on either Wrecks Motors or Royal Finance (section 69(1)) as Wrecks Motors are agents of Royal Finance for this purpose. If he posts the notice it need only be posted on the fifth day. It does not matter whether it arrives at all provided John can prove he posted it in time. The effect of cancellation is to cancel the agreement and any linked transaction (section 69(1)). Although the insurance is a linked transaction within section 19, being in compliance with a term of the principal agreement, it is exempt from the cancellation provisions under the Consumer Credit (Linked Transactions) (Exemptions) Regulations 1983. Therefore, John will have to cancel the insurance policy separately. On cancellation the car, which was taken in part-exchange, must be returned within 10 days of cancellation, or the negotiator (Smith), must re-pay the part-exchange allowance of £1,800 to John (section 73). (Although any sum paid by John must also be repaid by the creditor, there is no evidence that John made any payment.) John is under a duty to restore the new car to the other party but need not deliver the goods (section 72), *i.e.* they must collect it. However, he will have a lien over the car for the part-exchange goods/allowance.

Throughout the pre-cancellation period John is under a duty to take reasonable care of the car (CCA 1974, s.72(3)) and therefore will have to recompense Royal Finance for the damage done to the car by his wife. For 21 days following cancellation John will still be under this duty (Consumer Credit Act, s.72(8)).

Therefore, on the facts John can get out of the agreement by cancelling and it will cost him nothing except for the damage to the car.

John could consider termination but it would be an extreme measure considering the disadvantages and totally unnecessary on the facts.

Although Smith made representations regarding the car there is not enough evidence for misrepresentations.

It is always worth checking whether both the creditor (Royal Finance) and the credit broker (Wreck Motors/Smith) are licensed, if either of them is not, the agreement cannot be enforced without a validating order from the Director General of Fair Trading (sections 40 and 149).

QUESTION 3

(a) Eric recently purchased a kettle from Scurrys. The kettle was advertised by the shop as being "100 per cent stainless steel". When his wife, Olive, used it, she suffered an electric shock and dropped the kettle on her new ceramic tiled floor. The kettle was dented, the floor ruined and Olive was quite badly burned necessitating hospital treatment and time off work.

   The kettle was marked "Made in Hong Kong especially for Scurrys". On analysis, the kettle was shown to be 80 per cent aluminium, 20 per cent stainless steel.

(b) He also purchased with cash a new hi-fi system for £250 from "Bargains". Eric had bought many items there over the years. The shop assistant had said, and a clause on the till receipt read, "all goods sold as seen; no refunds given under any circumstances". When Eric arrived home with the hi-fi system, he discovered that it would not work at all.

   Advise Eric on all his remedies under the civil and criminal law.

Answer

(a) When Eric purchased the kettle from Scurrys his consumer transaction was governed by the Sale of Goods Act 1979. However, the major bulk of any claim is going to be the injuries suffered by Olive who is not a party to the contract. Arguments can be put forward for attempting to make her a party to the contract (*Jackson v Horizon Holidays* (1975)) but, as this could prove difficult, the way forward would be to use the Consumer Protection Act 1987. This Act, introduced as a result of a European Directive, regulates the law on defective products and creates strict liability so far as—

   (i) a manufacturer of goods is concerned;
   (ii) an own brander; or
   (iii) the first importer into the European Community.

The Act applies in respect of goods supplied after March 1, 1988 and the word "supplies" relates to the time the manufacturer supplied the goods to the retailer. Here, it would seem the time limits are satisfied, although of course checks would have to be made on this. Primary liability is cast upon the three people outlined above. Obviously, Scurrys are not a manufacturer but they could be classed as an own brander (who has held himself out as the producer). Judicial guidance is needed as to whether the words "made especially for Scurrys" mean that Scurrys are not holding themselves as a producer, at the moment some commentators feel that merely saying that "made especially for" will not allow own branders to escape liability. In any event, Scurrys will be liable as the first importer into the European Community. The Act imposes strict liability for damage caused by a defective product. This includes any personal injury damage and damage to private property totalling more than £275. Olive will therefore be able to claim for her personal injuries. There is no compensation under the Act for damage to the product itself (section 5) so nothing can be claimed for the kettle, this would have to be obtained by Eric using the Sale of Goods Act. As the kitchen is private property, this damage can be claimed under the Act.

As to the kettle not matching its description, there is an implied condition under section 13 of the Sale of Goods Act 1979 that the goods will correspond with their description. There has obviously been a breach of description, and as reliance was placed on it by Eric there can be no doubt it formed part of the description (*Harlingdon and Leinster v Christopher Hull Fine Art* (1991)). Eric is therefore entitled to reject the kettle subject to the doctrine of acceptance. Acceptance occurs by keeping the goods beyond a reasonable period of time and means that the condition in section 13 is reduced to a warranty (Sale of Goods Act, s.11(4)), for which damages only are payable. Eric must have been given a reasonable opportunity of examining the goods to see that they conform to the contract before acceptance occurs. Because Eric was dealing as a consumer, he is also entitled to exercise his rights to the four additional remedies under Section 48 of the Sale of Goods Act. The remedy of replacement might satisfy Eric although this is unlikely given the circumstances! Also, as the sellers were acting in the course of a business, because the goods were falsely described, an offence may have been committed under section 1 of the Trade Descriptions Act 1968. Clearly, there has been a false trade description and section 1 creates a strict liability offence subject only to defences set out in section 24 of the Act.

(b) The transaction here is covered by the Sale of Goods Act 1979. By section 14 of the Sale of Goods Act there is an implied condition that where the goods are sold in the course of a business they will be of satisfactory quality and will be reasonably fit for their purpose. These conditions also apply to the sale of second hand goods made in the course of a business, although the price paid is a very relevant factor in deciding whether or not the goods are of satisfactory quality. (See, *e.g. Bartlett v Sidney Marcus* (1965).) Here, as the hi-fi system does not work at all there would appear to be a breach of both conditions thereby entitling Eric to reject the system and get his money back. The notice on the till and on the receipt are exclusion clauses.

The first point to be considered is whether or not, by the common law rules, the clauses have been incorporated in the contract. Assuming their prominent position, incorporation appears to have taken place, and the clauses are therefore governed by the UCTA. The clause is trying to exclude liability for section 14 of the Sale of Goods Act. The effect of the UCTA, section 6, is that any clause that purports to do this is void where the buyer is dealing as a consumer. Is Eric dealing as a consumer? By section 6 of the UCTA, a person deals as a consumer where he buys from someone acting in the course of a business (*i.e.* Bargains) and he does not hold himself out as acting in the course of a business, (*i.e.* Eric is a private buyer). Eric is therefore dealing as a consumer, the clause is void and Eric is entitled to reject the goods and recover his money. The clauses would also be unfair under the Unfair Consumer Contract Regulations 1999. By contacting the Office of Fair Trading, Bargains could be instructed to alter these unfair terms. Eric could also pursue a civil remedy under the regulations.

In addition, by virtue of the Consumer Transactions (Restrictions on Statement) Order 1976, a trader can be guilty of a criminal offence where he exhibits a void exclusion clause in a notice or till receipt. Bargains could therefore be guilty of a criminal offence.

Once the exclusion clause has been disposed of, then as this is a non-severable contract, if acceptance has occurred then by section 11(4) of the Sale of Goods Act, the condition becomes a warranty for which damages only are payable. Here, as Eric is returning the goods immediately, there can be no question of acceptance. If, however, Eric wanted to exercise his rights to a replacement rather than a refund he could choose this. As the goods are not six months old, there is a presumption they were defective on delivery.

QUESTION 4

Mrs Smith purchased a radio cassette player for £149.99 from the Meteor Discount Store. She paid using her Bisa credit card. Three weeks later the radio cassette player stopped working. When Mrs Smith returned to the store she discovered it had closed down and all enquiries were to be addressed to the receiver "Draggit & Co.". Advise her.

Answer

Mrs Smith had a contract governed by the Sale of Goods Act 1979 with the Meteor Store. Implied into the contract are conditions under section 14 of the Act that the goods are of satisfactory quality and reasonably fit for their purpose as Meteor were selling in the course of a business.

As the radio cassette player broke down after three weeks there appears to be a breach of sections 14(2) and 14(3), assuming no user fault. As these are conditions, Mrs Smith would be entitled to reject the goods and obtain a full refund. She could exercise her rights to a replacement, should she choose. As only a three-week period has elapsed, the question of acceptance should not arise. As the Meteor Store has gone into liquidation, Mrs Smith can exercise her rights against Bisa by virtue of section 75 of the Consumer Credit Act.

This is because:

(a) By using her credit card, she has created a three-party debtor-creditor-supplier agreement for restricted use credit.

(b) The cash price of the goods is between £100 and £30,000. Here it was £150.00.
[**Note:** Section 75 would not apply if the goods had been priced at under £100.]

(c) The agreement must be regulated under the Consumer Credit Act 1974 so the card must be of the Mastercard or Visa variety and not one like Diners Club or American Express.

Under section 75, if Mrs Smith has a claim in contract against Meteor, she will have a like claim against Bisa. Her claim in contract results from a claim under section 14 of the Sale of Goods Act. If she has not paid the account yet she should decline to do so using section 75 as a shield.

INDEX

CREDIT TRANSACTIONS—*cont.*
  hire purchase—*cont.*
    exclusion clauses, 39
    implied terms, 22–3
    meaning, 51
    sample question and model
      answer, 113–16
  inability to pay
    extortionate bargains, 82–3
    generally, 78
    protected goods, 81–2
    termination, 78–81
    time orders, 81
  licensing
    requirements and sanctions, 64–5
    statutory provisions, 63–4
  loan-linked agreements, 54
  overdrafts, 55
  personal loans, 54–5
  regulated agreements
    DC or DCS agreements, 59–61
    defined, 55–6
    exemptions, 61–2
    linked transactions, 62–3
    monetary limits, 56
    restricted or unrestricted use, 58
    sample question and model
      answer, 116–19
  scope, 50
  statutory regulation, 49–50
  withdrawal, 67
CRIMINAL LIABILITY
  exclusion clauses, 45
  food safety
    defences, 105
    failure to comply with safety
      requirements, 102–3
    misrepresentation, 103–4
    punishment, 101
    rendering food injurious to
      health, 102
    statutory provisions, 100–1
  trade descriptions
    burden of proof, 86, 90
    business sales, 87–8
    defences, 95–7
    exclusion clauses, 88–90
    holidays, 92–5
    points to note, 90–2
    punishment, 87
    service contracts, 90
    statutory provisions, 86–7
  unsafe goods
    defences, 100
    manufacturers and distributors,
      99–100

CRIMINAL LIABILITY—*cont.*
  unsafe goods—*cont.*
    minimal risks, 99
    punishment, 100
    statutory provisions, 97–8
    suppliers, 99

DAMAGE, product liability, 31
DAMAGES
  distress and disappointment, 21–2
  sale of goods
    consequential losses, 20–1
    higher pricing and delay, 21
  service contracts, 26
DEATH
  exclusion clauses, 48
  product liability, 31
DEFECTIVE GOODS. *See also* PRODUCT
    LIABILITY; SALE OF GOODS
  credit transactions
    conditional sales, 74
    credit cards, 75–6
    hire purchase, 74
    linked transactions, 76–7
    overdraft purchases, 73–4
    personal loans, 77
  hire agreements, 84
DEFENCES
  food safety, 105
  misleading prices, 109
  product liability, 32–4
  unsafe goods, 100
DELIVERY, sale by description, 4–5
DESCRIPTION. *See* SALE BY DESCRIPTION
DISCLAIMERS. *See* EXCLUSION CLAUSES
DISCLOSURE, defective goods, 11
DISTRESS AND DISAPPOINTMENT
  defective goods, 21–2
  holidays, 92–5
  service contracts, 26
DISTRIBUTORS, unsafe goods, 99–100
DURABILITY, sale of goods, 7–9

ENFORCEMENT, unsafe goods, 100
EXAMINATION
  acceptance, 16
  defective goods, 11
EXAMINATION CHECKLIST, 111–13
EXCHANGE OF GOODS, implied terms, 24
EXCLUSION CLAUSES
  criminal liability, 45
  hire agreements, 84
  incorporation, 35–7
  misrepresentation, 45